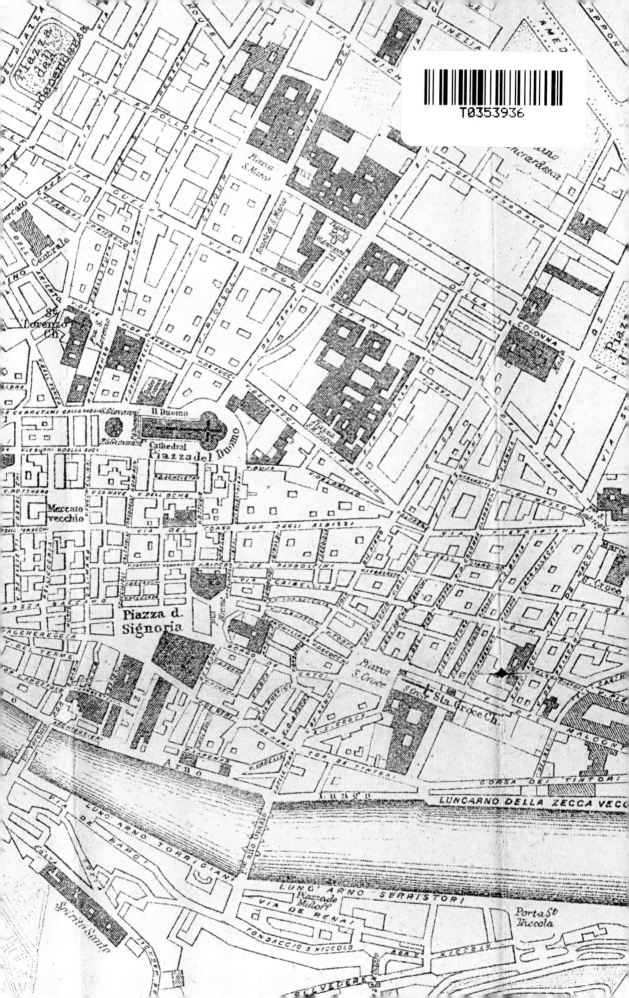

BRUTTO

This book is dedicated to my children
Oliver, Robin and Mabel

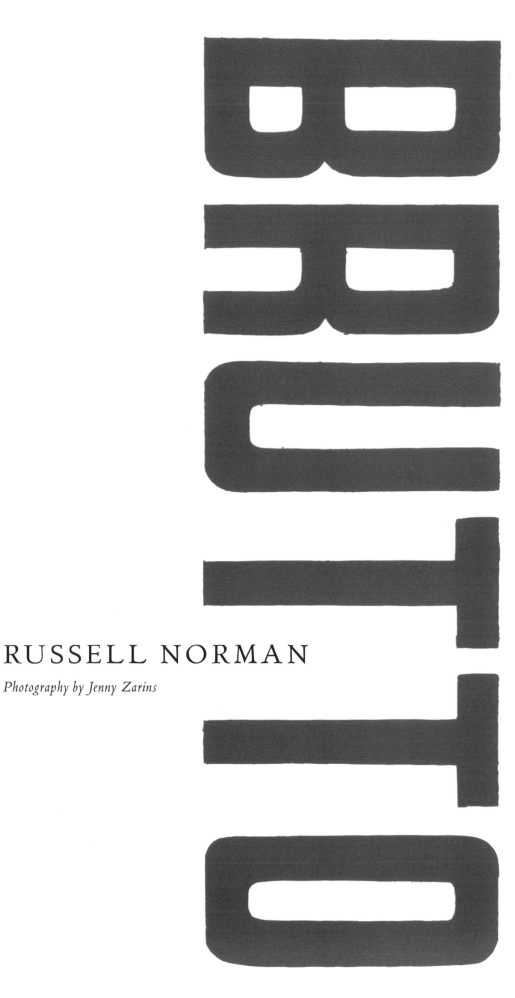

BRUTTO

RUSSELL NORMAN

Photography by Jenny Zarins

EBURY
PRESS

INTRODUCTION *14*

ANTIPASTI & SPUNTINI *22*

PRIMI *62*

INSALATE *108*

SECONDI *136*

CONTORNI *174*

BRODI, SALSE,
PASTE & DISPENSA *198*

DOLCI *230*

BEVANDE *266*

GAZETTEER *286*

INDEX *306*

ACKNOWLEDGEMENTS *313*

When I decided to call my restaurant B R U T T O it raised some eyebrows. *Brutto* is the Italian word for 'ugly', after all, and who in their right mind would want to call a restaurant U G L Y? I had my reasons.

Firstly, I liked the shape of the word, *brutto*. It has a strong appearance on the page and I knew it would look good on a shopfront and, crucially, when written in red capital letters on the lantern I had always envisaged hanging above the door. Secondly, it was easy for English speakers to pronounce. When spoken, those two syllables are like little punches, and the vowel sounds 'ooh' and 'oh' are, to the ear, like an expression of delight. Thirdly, I wholeheartedly endorsed its secondary meanings. Brutal. Inelegant. Basic. Unrefined. These all appealed to my notions of unfussiness and honesty when it comes to food. And, finally, because I loved the Italian expression *brutto ma buono* – 'ugly but good'. It's a phrase that is often used to describe the sort of cooking you might find in a family home, prepared lovingly by a grandmother, rough around the edges, unreconstructed on the plate, scant attention to fancy presentation and prettiness, but, *my god*, does it taste good …

Don't get me wrong – I love beautiful things too. Standing in front of Michelangelo's *David* at the Accademia in Florence, one of the most stunning artworks in the entire history of human endeavour, I have been known to shed a tear or two. But I'm drawn to imperfection and flaws, and I find a great deal of beauty in that which others might consider ugly. There is an expression in French – *jolie laide* – which describes that rare quality of ugly / beauty. The best type of beauty is the ugly type, obviously.

I was also very conscious of the irony and juxtaposition of creating a restaurant that would be gorgeous to look at, full of exquisite detail, with great lighting, beautiful fixtures and fittings, antiques, fabrics and tableware, but would also be peddling the idea that it was somehow ugly. Many people saw through my ploy and got the joke. B R U T T O was anything but *brutto*.

In terms of the design, I had started with just one image in my mind. There is a venerable and cherished *pensione* and *trattoria* in Venice called Antica Locanda Montin. It's off the beaten track by some margin, on a little canal that connects Campo San Barnaba with the Zattere. In order to attract passers-by, a large lantern hangs outside, the name of the restaurant painted in red letters on opaline glass panes. At night, it glows to attract customers like an angler fish attracts prey in the depths of the ocean. I found an antique, mid-nineteenth-century copper street-light in Paris, the metal turned verdigris green, brought it back to London, and did the same. Big red letters, illuminated by a single bulb through milky white glass. The site I had chosen for B R U T T O was on a dark, dead-end alleyway. The lamp seemed to work. The restaurant and bar were packed from opening day and B R U T T O continues to heave with happy drinkers and diners. This has much to do with the food, of course. But never underestimate a good lamp.

However, the story of B R U T T O begins not in Venice, but in Florence.

In 1817, Marie-Henri Beyle, better known as Stendhal, visited Florence for the first time. A French philosopher and novelist, he was used to experiencing culture, art and architecture in all its highest forms, but something weird happened that day. As he stepped out of a church in the city centre, he described it like this:

> 'As I emerged from the porch of Santa Croce, I was seized with a fierce palpitation of the heart … The well-spring of life was dried up within me, and I walked in constant fear of falling to the ground.'

We have come to refer to this phenomenon, thanks to the Italian psychiatrist Dr Graziella Magherini, as Stendhal Syndrome – a stupefying response to the overwhelming abundance of beauty. Many visitors to Florence have felt the same. I'm pretty sure it's what E. M. Forster describes in *A Room with a View* when Lucy Honeychurch faints in Piazza Signoria, memorably captured by Helena Bonham Carter in the Merchant/Ivory movie of 1985. (I did the same in 2001 on my first trip to the city, but that might have been heat exhaustion and one too many tripe sandwiches.)

There is no question that Florence has the ability to blow the mind. Subsequent trips for me were about visiting the Uffizi, the Accademia, the churches, Pitti Palace, San Miniato, Fiesole and so on, but, of course, I always wanted to find the gritty city under the touristy surface. It didn't take me long.

A friend suggested I might like the area south of the River Arno, a district known as Oltrarno, and in particular the piazza of Santo Spirito. It was exactly what I was looking for. Genuine locals, going about their business, shopping at the neighbourhood food stalls, eating in humble *trattorie*. It was around this time that I got to know the local watering-holes. Not the fancy restaurants with their expensive tourist menus north of the Arno in the shadows of the Duomo and Santa Maria del Fiore, but family-run hostelries with a simple daily offering of local specialities and comfort classics. A little further west from Santo Spirito lies the sub-district of San Frediano, a charming residential area where the restaurants and bars in the streets around the eponymous church are just as authentic and homely. Santo Spirito and San Frediano both come under the banner of Oltrarno and residents are very proud of their location. I have often heard them say the same thing when talking about their differences from the more famous historical part of the city north of the river:

> 'Santa Maria Novella may be the centre of the city, but Oltrarno is Florence.'

FLORENCE

Florence is a small city. It was originally walled and you can see the remains of the huge gates and high walls at several points on the perimeter of the ancient boundaries. You could probably walk across the whole historical centre, east to west or north to south, in under an hour, and I would suggest you do exactly that if you get a chance to visit. Simply following a map to get to a gallery or museum will only offer you a glimpse of Florence. There is much to explore accidentally and spontaneously by getting lost. Try it. You will always be able to use the Arno as your navigational lodestone, bringing you back to the three central bridges of Ponte alla Carraia, Ponte Santa Trinita and the world-famous Ponte Vecchio. (In all my trips to Florence, I don't think I have ever used the other bridges either side of this trio.) The sprawling suburbs to the west and north-west towards Prato have little to offer except an IKEA megastore and retail parks.

Crossing the river is a joy, however. The Arno is a mighty waterway, wide and calm, offering breathtaking views of the hills that surround this valley. To the north you will see Fiesole, a Roman settlement dating from 2 BC and definitely worth a day-trip. It's a twenty-minute bus ride from the centre of Florence and boasts a beautiful amphitheatre and a small number of exquisite museums and churches. I once attended a wedding at Santa Maria Primerana with the wedding breakfast served at Villa San Michele, and I remember the views back towards the city being spectacular. To the south of the river is the church of San Miniato al Monte, a mere kilometre up the hill and only a fifteen-minute walk, also offering superb views. The church itself adjoins an Olivetan monastery and if you're at the church at 6 a.m. you can see and hear the monks practising their Gregorian chanting. Or go later for the twice-daily mass and hear the monks in full voice after their early morning rehearsals. In November 1966 the Arno burst its banks and rose by 5 metres, causing a catastrophic flood. There is a plaque on the wall of a building in Via del Parione on the northern side of the Carraia Bridge off Piazza Carlo Goldoni. It shows the height to which the floodwaters rose.

The city is made up of neighbourhoods, each with its distinct characteristics and personalities. Walking from Piazza della Signoria through the international high-end shopping district, full of fashion megabrands like Gucci, Armani and Prada, and then stumbling into the Piazza del Duomo and seeing the gob-smacker that is Santa Maria del Fiore, you'd be forgiven for needing to take a breath and sit down. But head further north to the area around the Central Market, and Florence becomes more practical and real. Ignore the countless tourist stalls selling snow globes, cheap statuettes of Michelangelo's *David* and thousands of leather belts, handbags and purses, and pop into Casa del Vino (page 292) on Via dell'Ariento for a glass of local wine, or head over the road to my favourite catering goods shop, full of pots, pans, pasta-making hardware and specialist vegetable cutters you didn't know you needed. (You're also close to Nerbone in the Central Market itself (page 296). Their *lampredotto* is hard to resist.)

But head south and cross the River Arno again to Piazza Santo Spirito, and Florence changes its character dramatically. I could happily sit here all morning in the warm sun, reading Italo Calvino, drinking coffee and watching the city come to life.

Tuscan cooking is unique among the twenty regions of Italy, known for its reliance on meat, offal, game and beans. In fact, Tuscans are affectionately referred to throughout Italy as *mangiafagioli* – bean eaters. But the culinary traditions of this region have their origins in *cucina povera*, peasant cooking, which means there are also lots of vegetables, tomatoes, herbs and bread, those inexpensive ingredients that are easy to grow and make at home in rural areas and cheap to pick up at urban markets, too.

The other important ingredient is simplicity. You will often find that dishes consist of a single element plus the addition of pantry essentials such as salt, pepper, olive oil and herbs. Slow-cooked cannellini with sage or rosemary appears absolutely everywhere, in the *trattorie* and in domestic kitchens equally. Sliced Costoluto tomatoes with extra virgin olive oil and salt could not be simpler or more delicious in the summer months. And no self-respecting Tuscan cook would ever throw away stale bread. It has a multitude of uses, notably in classic *panzanella*, *ribollita* or *pappa al pomodoro*.

What I found in Florence was a meat-heavy tradition with a nose-to-tail philosophy. Nothing is wasted. The predominance of tripe – all four stomachs of the cow – has been a feature of the city's cooking for centuries and it shows no sign of changing any time soon. The popular street tripe stalls around the Central Market north of Santa Maria Novella often have crowds of hungry locals in the morning, and the historic Nerbone (page 296), in the market itself, does a roaring trade in *lampredotto*, *bollito* and *porchetta* from 8 a.m. to well past lunchtime. The almost complete absence of fish from the Florentine canon can be frustrating for pescatarian visitors to the city, but the nearest coast at Livorno is quite a schlep and, well, I suppose you must travel closer to the sea if you want fish. Vegetarians are somewhat better catered for, but with a caveat: often there will be nothing on a traditional *trattoria* menu for veggies other than soup, beans, tomatoes, cabbage and potatoes. A vegetarian friend was once given a plate of raw, un-podded broad beans when she asked for the 'vegetarian option' at a famous restaurant.

I've included many recipes that are a bit kinder to non-meat eaters while still giving an honest account of the region's flavours and traditions. (It may surprise you to learn that at BRUTTO around 40% of the menu is suitable for veggies.)

ANTIP
SP

Antipasti is a word derived from the Latin *ante* meaning 'before' and *pasti* meaning 'food' or 'a meal'. It has nothing to do with pasta, as many assume. An Italian friend likened *antipasti* to foreplay or the opening credits sequence of a movie. They are designed to whet your appetite and get you ready for the feast to come.

They can be shared, or eaten individually if, like Joey from *Friends*, you don't do sharing. They can also be incredibly simple – cold cuts of cured meat, a few cheeses and pickled vegetables, marinated fish from the deli, olives. But they can be a little more artful, too, combining strong flavours to create dishes that are more than the sum of their individual parts, like the smooth, loose chicken liver paté so beloved of Florentines and served virtually everywhere, in restaurants, bars, *trattorie* and homes across the region in as many iterations as there are days in a month.

Quite often the dishes in this section are all you will find in the city's wine bars. They are the go-to snack of the discerning drinker, small enough not to spoil your appetite but substantial enough to stop you getting too merry on an empty stomach. After all, as they say in Italy: *L'appetito vien mangiando* – 'Eating makes you hungry.'

At the table, it is important not to skip this part of the classic four-course tradition of most Italian regions. *Antipasti* provide a perfect reason to enjoy something bitter to drink, like a Negroni, a glass of vermouth or a Campari with soda before the wine.

ASTI &

JNTINI

ANCHOVIES, COLD BUTTER & SOURDOUGH
Acciughe, burro e pane

The British chef Shaun Hill famously replied, when asked the secret to good cooking: 'Buy the best ingredients and don't fuck it up.' This simple bar snack antipasto *requires the best of everything. Excellent Cantabrian or Sicilian tinned anchovies, the best unsalted butter, and very good, fresh sourdough or Tuscan unsalted bread.*

In Florence, the first time I had this dish was at Casa del Vino (page 292) next to the Central Market, where it was prepared in front of me by the bartender. They serve a great version at Alla Vecchia Bettola (page 292), too. Their charmingly kitsch presentation of curled butter appealed to my retro sensibilities and I reproduce it here.

For four to six:
2 or 3 slices of very good sourdough bread
12 excellent anchovy fillets
a pack of unsalted butter (but you won't use it all)

Toast the sourdough until golden brown. Set aside in a toast rack to cool completely. When cooled, slice into 12 lozenge-shaped fingers.

Remove the anchovies from the oil in the tin or jar. (Keep the oil for the tonnato sauce on pages 32–3.) Place on a plate. Add a few drops of the oil if they are looking dry.

Using a butter curler, or an old-fashioned jelly spoon, pull the tool across the top of the butter, straight from the fridge, to create 6 curls and plunge them into iced water.

When ready to serve, arrange the cold toasted sourdough fingers, the fillets and cold butter curls on a very large plate, board or platter. Provide butter knives for your guests to assemble the ingredients themselves.

CHICKEN LIVER CROSTINI OR 'BLACK TOASTS'

Crostini di fegatini di pollo o 'crostini neri'

In Tuscany, crostini *means this dish. It's sometimes referred to as* crostini neri — *black toasts — but everyone always assumes it's this funky, offaly chicken liver unless specified otherwise. And it rarely is.*

There are as many recipes as there are households and restaurants in Florence. Sometimes it's chunky and coarse. Sometimes it's wet and smooth. Often it's like paté. Occasionally it's like a liquid.

Please note that at B R U T T O we use chicken fat to sauté the shallots, but I'm aware this isn't always convenient or available in a domestic kitchen so I have substituted goose fat. You can use olive oil and still get a perfectly delicious result. The flavour that comes from the chicken livers and Marsala is quite convincing whichever frying medium you use.

For four to six:
300g chicken livers, cleaned with the bitter white bits removed
300ml whole milk
1 heaped tablespoon goose fat or 2 tablespoons extra virgin olive oil
2 shallots, finely chopped
flaky sea salt
4 sage leaves
1 teaspoon rosemary leaves
1 teaspoon thyme leaves
1 teaspoon capers
3 anchovy fillets
100ml white wine
50ml Marsala
a baguette, sliced into 12 × 2cm discs, toasted

One day before, cover the cleaned chicken livers with milk in a bowl and leave in the fridge overnight. When you're ready to cook the next day, drain the livers and discard the milk (or give it to your dog).

Heat the goose fat or olive oil in a large pan and gently sauté the shallots with a pinch of salt over a low to medium heat until glossy and soft. While the shallots are cooking, finely chop the herbs, capers and anchovies, then add to the pan and continue to sauté and stir for another few minutes. Add a little olive oil if necessary.

Pour in the white wine and turn up the heat to a bubble until the liquid is reduced by about a half. Now add the drained livers and fry until they colour, about 4–5 minutes, and are incorporated into the shallot and herb mixture. Reduce the heat and continue to cook for a further 10 minutes, continuing to stir.

When most of the liquid has been absorbed or has evaporated, take off the heat for 5 minutes and then put the contents of the pan into a blender. Pulse for 30 seconds. The mixture should have a thick, mousse-like consistency. Pour and spoon the contents of the blender into a clean pan, place on a low heat, taste and add more salt if necessary. Add the Marsala and continue to heat and gently stir until it looks smooth and spreadable.

Allow to cool for 5 minutes, then spread the warm mixture on to your 12 toasts.

CANNELLINI & OREGANO CROSTINI

Crostini con cannellini e origano

This is a vegetarian alternative to the classic Florentine chicken liver crostini neri but which stays true to the regional reliance on beans.

For four to six:
1 large ripe tomato, halved
a handful of fresh sage leaves, tied in a bunch
1 bay leaf
2 plump rosemary sprigs
1 clove of garlic
250g dried cannellini beans, soaked in cold water overnight
a handful of fresh oregano leaves, no stalks, chopped
flaky sea salt
extra virgin olive oil
a baguette, sliced into 12 × 2cm discs

Bring a pan of water to the boil with the tomato, bunched sage, bay leaf, rosemary sprigs and the garlic clove. Once boiling, add the drained cannellini beans, reduce the heat, cover and simmer for 1 hour. Remove and discard the sage and rosemary. Add the chopped oregano. Simmer for a further 20 minutes.

Drain the beans, garlic, tomato and oregano, discarding the tomato skins and bay leaf, and mash together in a large bowl with a wooden spoon or a masher. Add a couple of good pinches of sea salt and a glug or two of olive oil. You can use an electric blender if you prefer. Taste and adjust the seasoning if necessary. Set aside.

Lightly grill the 12 slices of baguette on both sides. Stir the smooth bean mixture once or twice, then generously load on to the crostini. Drizzle with olive oil and serve.

PORK WITH TUNA SAUCE & CAPERBERRIES
Maiale tonnato con bacche di capperi

The classic Piedmontese dish vitello tonnato *appears all over Italy and in many Italian restaurants around the world. In my experience the international versions tend to involve a tuna sauce that is often very loose and which completely covers the delicate slices of veal, rather like a fishy gravy. I'm not a fan.*

Substituting the veal with thinly sliced roasted pork loin and being a bit Jackson Pollock with a stiffer tuna sauce, however, makes it much more appealing in my opinion. This is closer to the versions I have eaten in Florence and, dare I say, is an improvement on the original.

For four:
400g free-range, outdoor-reared pork loin
extra virgin olive oil
flaky sea salt
black pepper

For the sauce:
50g tinned tuna chunks in oil, drained (but reserve the oil)
5 tinned anchovy fillets (keep the oil from the tin)
1 teaspoon Dijon mustard
1 heaped teaspoon capers
1 tablespoon lemon juice
flaky sea salt
black pepper
extra virgin olive oil

To garnish:
16 caperberries
a small handful of flat parsley leaves, roughly chopped

Roast the pork the day before, or at least 2 or 3 hours ahead of when you want to prepare and serve the dish.

Preheat the oven to 160°C. Massage the pork loin all over with olive oil and lots of salt and pepper. Heat a tablespoon of olive oil in a large, heavy-based frying pan and place the loin in the hot oil. Keep turning the pork until it is nicely brown on all sides. Remove the pan from the heat and transfer the loin into a roasting tin, add a splash more oil and a pinch more salt and place in the oven.

Roast for around 20–25 minutes, less if you like your pork pink, as I do. (If it's free-range and outdoor-reared, there's no need to follow the 1950s obsession with always cooking good pork well-done.) Turn once at the halfway mark. Remove from the oven, allow to cool completely, then wrap tightly in foil and place in the fridge for at least 2 hours but preferably overnight.

To make the *tonnato* sauce, place the tuna, anchovies, mustard, capers, lemon juice, a pinch of salt, a twist of black pepper and the reserved fish oils from the tins in a blender. (If you have the anchovy oil you saved from page 27, use that too.) Pulse until you achieve a gloopy mayonnaise consistency, carefully adding a thin stream of olive oil if necessary. Taste, and add more salt if necessary.

Remove and discard the stalks from 8 of the caperberries, then slice them finely. Leave the other 8 intact.

Remove the pork from the fridge and, with an extremely sharp knife, slice the loin as thinly as possible. Divide the cold slices equally between four large, flat plates, then liberally distribute the tuna sauce on to the pork in the manner of your favourite Post-Expressionist painter. Scatter over the chopped caperberries and finish each plate with 2 intact ones, and a light flourish of chopped parsley. A final drizzle of olive oil will give a shiny glint just before serving.

RAW VEGETABLES WITH NEW-SEASON OLIVE OIL & LEMON

Pinzimonio

The olive oil makers of Tuscany harvest their crops in autumn. The first-press, new-season oil is highly prized and often very delicate. To taste it with bread would be considered an insult to such a subtle and nuanced product, and so raw vegetables are the preferred vehicle.

These days pinzimonio is served in restaurants as an example of a typical Tuscan | Roman antipasto but it's actually a rare culinary example of the tail wagging the dog: the oil came first, the main dish was just the support act.

For four:
2 fennel bulbs
1 head of celery, leafy, washed (optional)
8 baby heritage carrots, preferably different colours, peeled
8 assorted radishes
3 spring onions (optional)
200ml excellent extra virgin olive oil, preferably new-season
flaky sea salt
1 lemon

Remove the outer leaves of the fennel bulbs, trim any brown edges from the core, and slice lengthways into quarters or sixths, depending on size. Remove the outer stalks from the celery, remove the bottom third (perhaps reserve for a stock or *soffritto*) and slice the remaining leafy stalks lengthways into sixths. Cut the carrots and radishes in half, also lengthways. Trim the spring onions.

If you're not eating the vegetables straight away, you can submerge them in iced water with a few drops of lemon juice, but make sure you drain and dry them thoroughly.

Arrange the vegetables on a large platter. Lay four side plates each with a small bowl of 50ml of the extra virgin olive oil and a small mound of sea salt. Divide the lemon into four wedges and lay them on the side plates. Or you can plate everything individually as I have shown in the photograph opposite.

DOUGH BALL 'CUDDLES' WITH STRACCHINO & PROSCIUTTO

Coccoli

The British wine consultant Emily O'Hare, who lives and works in Siena, joined me for lunch at one of my favourite restaurants in Florence, I'Brindellone, (page 293) one sunny day in the summer of 2021. We sat outside: fuori in Italian, not the clumsy English 'al fresco' which actually translates as 'in the cool' or, colloquially, 'in prison'.

She saw coccoli on the menu and asked if I'd ever had them before. I had not. She explained that it was a simple dish of hot, fried dough balls which you split apart with your hands and fill with raw cow's milk stracchino soft cheese and a slice of prosciutto. She also pointed out that the Italian word for 'cuddles' was a near-homonym for coccoli: coccole.

I was sold. When I returned to Florence with BRUTTO head chef Oli Diver a month later we had coccoli again. 'We have to put this on the menu,' he said. I agreed.

It's one of our best-selling dishes.

For four:
800g simple bread dough (page 221)
'00' flour, for dusting
12 very thin slices of prosciutto
400g fresh *stracchino*
2 litres sunflower oil, for frying

Divide the dough into 16 small portions and roughly roll them into the shape of ping-pong balls. Dust lightly with the flour and allow them to expand slightly while covered loosely with oiled clingfilm. About 45 minutes to 1 hour.

Take the prosciutto and *stracchino* out of the fridge to bring them to room temperature. Pull the prosciutto slices apart, roughly in half, and divide the *stracchino* between four small ramekins.

Heat the oil in a large saucepan and bring up to around 180°C. Drop the dough balls into the hot oil (you may need to do this in batches, depending on the size of the pan) until they appear puffed up and golden brown – about 2 minutes or even less, depending on the temperature of the oil. (They will be too pale and soggy if the oil isn't hot enough, and burnt if it's too hot, so use a cooking thermometer if you can.)

Remove the cooked dough balls from the oil with a slotted spoon and let them rest on kitchen paper for a minute. Meanwhile, equally share the roughly torn prosciutto slices between four large plates and place a ramekin of *stracchino* on each. Finally put the hot, fried *coccoli* on to the plates and serve.

DEEP-FRIED COURGETTE FLOWERS

Fiori di zucchini fritti

This is a popular starter all over Italy and is quite often served with a cheese stuffing. But I prefer the simplicity of this version from Tuscany, where just the male flowers — the ones attached to the stem of the courgette plant, not the female flowers attached to the end of the young courgettes — are dipped into a rich batter and deep-fried.

For four:
250g '00' flour
5 tablespoons extra virgin olive oil
3 large free-range egg whites
1 litre vegetable oil, for frying
20 courgette flowers, stamens removed
flaky sea salt

Make the batter an hour before you want to start cooking.

Place the flour in a large bowl and add the olive oil to make a paste, stirring with a wooden spoon. Then slowly stir in warm water, a little at a time, until the mix has the consistency of thick batter, a little like double cream. Refrigerate for 1 hour.

Whisk the egg whites in a separate bowl until they have stiffened somewhat, then remove the flour and water mix from the fridge and fold in the egg whites until combined. Place the oil in a large saucepan on a high heat until it reaches 180°C. You can test by dropping a little batter in — it will turn brown in a few seconds.

Dip the flowers into the batter, shake off any excess, and place in the oil. You may need to do this in batches. They will turn golden brown and crisp in about 2–3 minutes. Remove on to kitchen paper with a slotted spoon, then transfer to a large platter and serve with a good sprinkling of sea salt flakes.

'GRANNY'S HANDKERCHIEFS', FLORENTINE SPINACH & RICOTTA PANCAKES
Crespelle

More often than not you will see these savoury pancakes on the primi *section of a trattoria menu, next to the pasta, soup and risotto. But I like to enjoy them as a snack — they're not quite finger food but you can easily polish one off with a fork in no time at all. Incidentally, you may think of béchamel sauce as being French in origin. Not so. Florence claims it was theirs first, known as* salsa colla *— 'glue sauce' — and was imported to France by Catherine de' Medici.*

I've heard crespelle *referred to as granny's handkerchiefs, probably because of the way they are folded rather than rolled.*

For eight to ten pancakes:
500g baby spinach leaves, thoroughly washed and drained
300g ricotta
3 medium free-range eggs
60g grated Parmesan
nutmeg
flaky sea salt
black pepper
180g '00' flour
600ml whole milk
100g butter, plus more for frying
100ml good tomato passata

Cook the spinach in a large saucepan on a medium heat with a mere splash of cold water. Keep turning it with a wooden spoon. The spinach will reduce quite substantially in about 2 minutes. When cooked, remove from the heat, allow to cool, then squeeze all the water out. You may need to do this two or three times. Chop finely.

Place the cooled, chopped spinach in a large mixing bowl along with the ricotta, one of the eggs, the grated Parmesan and a grating of nutmeg. Season with salt and black pepper and mix thoroughly. Set aside.

Make the pancake batter by putting 100g of the flour into a bowl with the other 2 eggs, 200ml of the milk, one quarter of the butter, melted, and a pinch of salt. Mix using an electric whisk, a manual whisk, or old-fashioned hard work with a wooden spoon. When it is completely smooth and lump-free, place in the fridge for at least 30 minutes.

For the béchamel sauce, melt the remaining butter in a pan on a low heat, add the rest of the flour and stir to create a yellow paste, then slowly introduce the remaining milk while stirring all the while to avoid lumps. You may not need to use all of it; pour in gradually and stir until you have a thick, creamy consistency. Add a small grating of nutmeg and cook on a very low heat for a further 10 minutes.

Preheat the oven to 180°C. Make 8–10 small pancakes in a non-stick frying pan using a little hot butter and a ladleful of the batter from the fridge. Flip once halfway through frying but don't overdo them. Set them aside until you've made them all, then spread the spinach mixture on one half of each. Fold the pancakes in half, then in half again to create little triangles.

Lay them on several greased baking sheets or ovenproof dishes. Generously cover the *crespelle* with the warm béchamel sauce, add a few splotches of passata and bake for 12–15 minutes until golden brown.

ANCHOVIES WITH ORANGE ZEST

Acciughe con scorza d'arancia

This is a gloriously simple snack that I hope will surprise and delight. I love the unexpected thrill you get when you try two flavours together and they do something alchemic that they can't achieve individually. The key, as always, is to use the best iteration of these ingredients and choose only excellent anchovies and excellent extra virgin olive oil. The little tins of anchovies you find in supermarkets can vary greatly in quality, but the best ones normally contain fat, wide fillets and yield about 10 to the tin. Don't use the oil from the tin on the plate – it is important to use the really good oil you have saved in your pantry for special occasions. (You can save the anchovy oil for the tonnato *recipe on page 32–3.)*

For four:
4 × 50g tins of excellent anchovies
2 oranges
your best extra virgin olive oil

Choose four wide, plain plates and arrange them in front of you. Open the tins of anchovies and lay the fillets in a straight row pointing upwards, like regiments of fishy soldiers. Be careful to drain them as you remove them, and pull them out slowly and carefully – they need to be intact on the plates, not broken and messy.

Using a zester, pull the tool across the surface of each orange to produce long strips of skin. It is important that you only remove the zest. If you hit the pith, you've gone too deep.

Lay the fronds of orange zest equally over the four portions of anchovies, drizzle a little of the extra virgin olive oil on to each plate, and serve with a strong drink like a Negroni or a Martini.

PEAR WITH PECORINO & TOASTED WALNUTS
Pera con cacio e noci

Do you know about pears and cheese? Fruit-growers in Italy who employ unskilled seasonal workers famously don't mention the magic of this combination, hoping that they won't lose too much of their crop to hungry pear-pickers who have packed a hunk of Pecorino in their knapsack for a midday snack.

Make sure you buy the plump Decana variety if you can. These pears are usually grown in the orchards around Modena and have a distinctive blob of red wax on the stalk. This is to stop them ripening too quickly. Another tip I would suggest is to leave the Pecorino at room temperature for half an hour so that it starts to sweat and properly develop in flavour.

For four:
400g walnut halves
extra virgin olive oil
4 ripe Decana pears
400g Pecorino

Preheat the oven to 180°C. Scatter the walnut halves on a large baking sheet, splash on a little olive oil, shake to coat lightly and toast in the oven for 10 minutes until just starting to darken, but keep an eye on them and make sure they don't burn. Remove and allow to cool slightly.

Remove the skin from the pears with a potato peeler, then slice them lengthways into strips, discarding the core.

Cut the Pecorino into similar-sized pieces.

Assemble the pears and Pecorino on four plates, scatter over the (still warm) walnuts and serve immediately.

TRIPE ROLLS
Panini con lampredotto

The legendary Central Market in Florence is a cathedral to meat in all its variations. You can choose to worship at the altar of the mighty bistecca alla fiorentina *(page 143) or spend time in the chancel, ogling the offal and, in particular, the tripe. Tripe is the washed stomach of the cow or, to be more accurate, the stomachs of the cow. They have four.*

Lampredotto is the fourth stomach, a brown and crinkly product that is softer and easier to cook than the feathery and honeycombed first three. The venerable market meat stall Nerbone (page 296) makes a simple crusty roll stuffed with stewed lampredotto *served with* salsa verde *and chilli and tomato sauce and it is excellent. Food pilgrims have been paying their respects at the sacristy in this corner of the market for decades. This is our version.*

For four panini:
800g *lampredotto* (ask your butcher for the fourth stomach of the cow)
extra virgin olive oil
1 medium onion, finely sliced
1 medium carrot, peeled and finely diced
1 celery stalk, finely diced
2 cloves of garlic, very finely chopped
1 heaped teaspoon chilli flakes
3 tablespoons tomato purée
200ml *brodo* (page 202), or beef stock
4 crusty white bread rolls
4 tablespoons *salsa verde* (page 210)

First wash the tripe in cold water, changing the water several times, until it is free from residue and the water remains clear. Drain, pat dry with kitchen paper, slice into short ribbons and set aside.

Heat 3 or 4 tablespoons of olive oil in a large, heavy-based saucepan for which you have a lid. Gently sauté the onion, carrot and celery until soft and translucent, around 15 minutes. Make sure the onion doesn't get brown or burnt. Add the chopped garlic and stir in for one minute, then add half the chilli flakes. Stir for one more minute, then introduce the sliced *lampredotto*. Turn up the heat slightly and fry the tripe with the other ingredients until just starting to brown. About 5 minutes. Add the tomato purée and stir for 1 more minute. Add the *brodo*, allow it to bubble, then cover and leave on a very low simmer for 1–1½ hours until reduced but not too dry. Halfway through, stir and add the rest of the chilli flakes. Test a small piece of *lampredotto* to make sure it's tender. Cook for longer if not.

Take off the heat, split open the crusty rolls, transfer the tripe mixture with a slotted spoon to the middle of the rolls and spoon over a little of the pan juices. Add a large dollop of *salsa verde* and serve with lots of paper napkins for the full Nerbone experience.

BAR PIZZAS
Pizze da bar

These savoury snacks sit in glass cabinets atop bakery counters and bars in Florence, usually cut into square or rectangular pieces that are easy to hold with one hand while you sip a beer or drink a coffee with the other. They are normally just a few euros each. Quite often local workers will order several to take away wrapped in parchment. They are frequently sold at room temperature when they've been sitting for more than 10 minutes but you will have the option of serving them hot if you prefer. I don't mind them cold at all. In fact, when there's any left over I will put them into the fridge overnight and have them straight from the chiller for breakfast the next morning.

TOMATO, MOZZARELLA & BASIL BAR PIZZA
Con pomodoro, mozzarella e basilico

The classic Margherita pizza topping. Just be sparing with the tomato layer and make sure the mozzarella isn't too wet, otherwise the pizza base will be soggy when cooked.

Makes six to eight little pizza slices:
extra virgin olive oil
½ the quantity of dough from page 221
flour, for dusting
4–6 tablespoons passata, a pinch of salt added
1 large ball of buffalo mozzarella, drained
a handful of basil leaves

Preheat the oven to its highest setting, usually 240–250°C for most domestic cookers. Drizzle a little oil on to your baking sheet and rub it in with your hands to cover the whole surface.

Roll and stretch the dough on a clean work surface, using a combination of your hands for gentle pulling and a rolling pin for flattening. Use a sprinkle of flour if the dough starts to stick. Don't worry too much if the sides look wonky. Make a rectangle the same size as your baking sheet. Place the pizza base on the baking sheet. (Alternatively, you can do this on the baking sheet, rolling and pushing the dough into the corners to make a rectangle.)

Evenly distribute the salted passata almost to the edges, leaving a 1cm border for the crust to form. Don't use all the passata if you've covered the surface with fewer spoonfuls. Less is more in this instance. Tear the mozzarella into small pieces and scatter equally.

Place in the oven on the middle shelf and check on it after 6 or 7 minutes. Turn it around or move it to the lower shelf if the cheese is already turning golden. Cook for a further 2–4 minutes if necessary, then remove, scatter with the basil leaves, cut into small, manageable slices and serve on a sheet of parchment as a snack.

POTATO, ROSEMARY & PECORINO BAR PIZZA
Con patate, rosmarino e Pecorino

A favourite combination of mine. The thinner the slices of waxy potato, the better the chance that some will turn golden and crisp in the oven, which is definitely what you want.

Makes six to eight little pizza slices:
extra virgin olive oil
2 waxy potatoes
½ the quantity of dough from page 221
flour, for dusting
100g Pecorino, grated
a small handful of rosemary leaves

Preheat the oven to its highest setting, usually 240–250°C for most domestic cookers. Drizzle a little oil on to your baking sheet and rub it in with your hands to cover the whole surface.

Boil a saucepan of water, slice the waxy potatoes very thinly, and plunge them into the boiling water for a maximum of 1 minute. Drain and rinse under a cold running tap.

Roll and stretch the dough on a clean work surface, using a combination of your hands for gentle pulling and a rolling pin for flattening. Use a sprinkling of flour if the dough starts to stick. Don't worry too much if the sides look wonky. Make a rectangle the same size as your baking sheet. Place the pizza base on the baking sheet. (Alternatively, you can do this on the baking sheet, rolling and pushing the dough into the corners to make a rectangle.)

Scatter most of the grated Pecorino over the dough, distribute the potato slices, then the rest of the grated cheese. Spread the rosemary evenly.

Place in the oven on the middle shelf and check on it after 6 or 7 minutes. Turn it around or move it to the lower shelf if the cheese is already turning golden. Cook for a further 2–4 minutes if necessary, remove, cut into small, manageable slices and serve on a sheet of parchment as a snack.

TOMATO, GARLIC & OREGANO BAR PIZZA
Marinara

It's a common mistake to think that a marinara *sauce has some sort of fish element. The name refers to the fact that it was favoured by sailors, not because of any marine ingredient.*

Makes six to eight little pizza slices:
1 clove of garlic, peeled
extra virgin olive oil
½ the quantity of dough from page 221
flour, for dusting
fine salt
6 tablespoons passata
1 tablespoon dried oregano

Using an extremely sharp knife, or even an old-school razor blade like in the prison cooking scene from Scorsese's *Goodfellas*, slice the garlic clove as finely as possible.

Preheat the oven to its highest setting, usually 240–250°C for most domestic cookers. Drizzle a little oil on to your baking sheet and rub it in with your hands to cover the whole surface.

Roll and stretch the dough on a clean work surface, using a combination of your hands for gentle pulling and a rolling pin for flattening. Use a sprinkling of flour if the dough starts to stick. Don't worry too much if the sides look wonky. Make a rectangle the same size as your baking sheet. Place the pizza base on the baking sheet. (Alternatively, you can do this on the baking sheet, rolling and pushing the dough into the corners to make a rectangle.)

Add a pinch of salt to the passata and stir. If it's looking a bit watery (some varieties are wetter than others), drain using a sieve. Spread the sauce over the dough, leaving a 1cm gap at the edges to allow a crust to form when cooking. Scatter the finely sliced garlic and dried oregano evenly over the surface.

Place in the oven on the middle shelf and check on it after 6 or 7 minutes. Turn it around or move it to the lower shelf if it is looking too dry. Cook for a further 2–4 minutes if necessary, then remove, cut into small, manageable slices and serve on a sheet of parchment as a snack.

ANCHOVY & BLACK OLIVE BAR PIZZA
Con acciughe e olive nere

This is one of the very rare occasions in Italian cuisine when you are permitted to combine fish with cheese, normally extremely frowned upon. Use the cheap, yellow, rubbery mozzarella, not the fancy milky white type.

Makes six to eight little pizza slices:
a large handful of Taggiasca olives, pitted
$1 \times 50g$ tin of anchovies
extra virgin olive oil
½ the quantity of dough from page 221
flour, for dusting
4 tablespoons passata, a pinch of salt added
2 large handfuls of grated mozzarella

Roughly chop the pitted olives and set aside. Drain the tin of anchovies and carefully remove the fillets. There are normally around 10.

Preheat the oven to its highest setting, usually 240–250°C for most domestic cookers. Drizzle a little oil on to your baking sheet and rub it in with your hands to cover the whole surface.

Roll and stretch the dough on a clean work surface, using a combination of your hands for gentle pulling and a rolling pin for flattening. Use a sprinkling of flour if the dough starts to stick. Don't worry too much if the sides look wonky. Make a rectangle the same size as your baking sheet. Place the pizza base on the baking sheet. (Alternatively, you can do this on the baking sheet, rolling and pushing the dough into the corners to make a rectangle.)

Smear the passata on to the dough, leaving a 1cm gap at the edges. Scatter over the grated mozzarella. Distribute the olives and anchovies evenly.

Place in the oven on the middle shelf and check on it after 6 or 7 minutes. Turn it around or move it to the lower shelf if the cheese is already turning golden. Cook for a further 2–4 minutes if necessary, then remove, cut into small, manageable slices and serve on a sheet of parchment as a snack.

PR

I think the *primi* course of the traditional Italian meal is the one that causes non-Italians the most confusion. You've had your starter (UK) or appetizer (US) and now there's a further round of food between those and the main dish. What's happening? And it's all *heavy carbohydrate*: pasta, rice or bread-based soups …

The trick is to follow Italian portion sizes. *Primi* in Italy are never served as mounds of starch as they are in international doses. And the course that follows the *primi* rarely has a vegetable and / or potato accompaniment. It's usually a single element of protein. The balance works if you adhere to proper traditions.

Having said that, at lunchtime in particular, many regional cuisines stop at this course, so you can still function in the afternoon and save some appetite for dinner.

TAGLIATELLE
WITH MEAT SAUCE
Tagliatelle al ragù

The classic meat sauce (ragù or sugo, depending on where you are) is debated and discussed endlessly. Beef or pork? Both? Herbs or not? Garlic or not? Red wine or white wine? Milk or no milk? There is no right answer and there will never be a consensus. It sparks fierce passion and disagreement.

BRUTTO's senior sous chef Alan Williams worked in Bologna for three years and we make his traditional Emilia-Romagna version. He insists that you can't do justice to this recipe in under 6 hours, but I've adapted it for a domestic kitchen. It's the best ragù *I've tasted.*

For four:
30g pork fat (or lard)
200g beef mince
200g pork mince
flaky sea salt
black pepper
300ml white wine
1 large onion, very finely diced
2 medium carrots, peeled and very finely diced
2 celery stalks, very finely diced
extra virgin olive oil
200ml whole milk
1 × 400g tin of good quality chopped tomatoes
200ml chicken stock (more to top up if necessary) (page 205)
320g fresh tagliatelle
120g grated Parmesan, for serving

Now this may surprise you: we are going to cook the meat first.

In a very large, heavy-bottomed saucepan, heat the pork fat (or lard) and sauté the beef and pork mince, with a good pinch of salt and a hearty twist of black pepper, for about 10 minutes until the meat has turned nicely brown. Keep stirring. If the meat starts to stick to the pan, add a good splash of white wine and stir some more. (The cheffy term is 'deglaze'.)

Remove the meat and set aside. Add the onion, carrot and celery to the same pan, with a splash of olive oil and a pinch more salt, and sauté until soft and translucent, about 10–15 minutes. Deglaze with some more wine if it starts to stick. Now return the meat to the pan along with the milk, tomatoes, chicken stock and the remaining wine. Bubble away on a low heat for 2 hours (6 if you're Alan) until the sauce achieves a jammy, lava-like consistency. Top up with a little more stock if it's getting too dry.

Cook the fresh tagliatelle in salted, boiling water for 3–4 minutes until *al dente*, but not too soft. Reserve a cup of the cooking water. Drain the pasta and combine with the sauce. Use the pasta water if you need to loosen the sauce.

Serve with plenty of grated Parmesan.

PAPPARDELLE WITH RABBIT, LEMON & HERBS

Pappardelle con coniglio, limone e erbe

*Tuscany is a rural region, with many plains, fields, hills, forests and farmsteads between the major cities of Florence, Pisa and Siena. It comes as no surprise, then, that game and wildfowl feature heavily in the culinary canon. Wild boar (*chingale*) are almost like vermin, running across country roads and squealing at night while you're trying to read Primo Levi with a nice glass of Chianti. First world problems, eh? Fortunately the rabbits are quiet, and they are plentiful and very cheap. And delicious. Wild rabbit is best, of course, and if you can find an off-grid loner like Jake the poacher from* Withnail & I *with a string of leporidae across his back, all the better. But even the French farmed versions will work in this dish.*

For four:
8 rabbit legs, skinned and cleaned
flaky sea salt
extra virgin olive oil (or chicken fat)
500ml chicken stock (page 205)
2 large onions, very finely chopped
2 large carrots, peeled and very finely chopped
2 celery stalks, very finely chopped
1 clove of garlic, very finely sliced
200ml white wine
1 bay leaf
a bunch of rosemary, tightly tied with string
a handful of thyme leaves, no stalks, chopped
320g fresh pappardelle
a large knob of butter
the juice and zest of ½ a lemon
a handful of parsley leaves, finely chopped
grated Parmesan, for serving
black pepper

Season the rabbit legs with salt and place them in a large, hot frying pan with 2 large tablespoons of chicken fat or olive oil. Make sure they are brown all over – 5 minutes should do it. Place them in a large roasting tin in a single layer and set aside. Put the chicken stock into a pan on the back of the hob and bring to a gentle simmer. Preheat the oven to 180°C.

Using the same, unwashed frying pan in which you cooked the rabbit, sauté the onion, carrot, celery and garlic in a splash more olive oil with a pinch of salt on a low heat until soft and glossy, about 12–15 minutes. Turn up the heat. Add the wine, the bay leaf, the tied rosemary sprigs and the chopped thyme. Reduce the liquid by a third and then pour everything over the rabbit legs in the roasting tray. Cover with the bubbling stock from the back of the stove, then wrap the tray in foil. Place in the oven for 1 hour.

After an hour, check to see if the rabbit flesh can be pulled or forked away from the bones easily. If not, put back into the oven, covered, for a bit longer until it can. When ready, allow to cool somewhat, then pull the meat from the bones, discarding any bone or gristle. Also discard the bay leaf and the rosemary. Put the pulled flesh back into the tray with the vegetables and reduced stock.

Cook the pappardelle in salted boiling water for 3–4 minutes until *al dente* but not soft, then drain and combine with the rabbit sauce. Add the knob of butter, the lemon juice and zest, and the finely chopped parsley and heat briefly while stirring on a high heat. Keep a small cup of the pasta cooking water to add to the final mix to bind the sauce with the pasta.

Serve on four warmed plates, with plenty of Parmesan and black pepper.

PASTA, BORLOTTI BEAN & ROSEMARY SOUP
Pasta e fagioli

When I think of comfort food, my mind turns to pasta e fagioli. *It's a very good example of a dish that may not look pretty, but delivers a lot of flavour and satisfying umami. The ingredients are inexpensive and it's a very reliable pantry staple — you should have pretty much everything you need in your larder and fridge without needing to go shopping.*

You can use any small pasta shape but ditalini or macaroni work best. The quantities in this recipe will serve more than four people but I like the option of going back for seconds.

For four:
extra virgin olive oil
125g unsmoked pancetta, cut into small matchsticks
1 clove of garlic, finely chopped
1 medium onion, finely diced
1 medium carrot, peeled and finely diced
1 celery stalk, finely diced
250g dried borlotti beans, soaked overnight in cold water
a handful of rosemary leaves, no stalks
1.5 litres hot chicken stock (page 205)
200g ditalini
flaky sea salt
black pepper
grated Parmesan, for serving
crusty bread, for serving

Place a large saucepan on a medium heat and add a good glug or two of olive oil. Gently sauté the pancetta for a couple of minutes until the meat is starting to colour. Add the chopped garlic and stir for a further minute. Now add the onion, carrot and celery and a splash more olive oil. Coat all the ingredients well and sweat for 12 minutes or so, until glossy and translucent.

Drain and rinse the borlotti beans. Add them to the pan with the rosemary, stir for a few minutes, then add two-thirds of the chicken stock. Bring to a gentle boil, then reduce to a low simmer, cover with the lid and leave for 2 hours.

Remove about half the beans with a slotted spoon and place them in a blender. When the mixture has a thick, smooth consistency, return it to the pan and add the pasta and the rest of the stock if necessary, with a good pinch of salt and a twist of black pepper. Cook for a further 5–6 minutes, taste and add more salt if needed, and serve in four warmed bowls. Zig-zag the top of each serving with a thin stream of olive oil, using a pourer or your thumb to stop the olive oil drizzling too quickly.

Serve with plenty of Parmesan on the table and some crusty bread.

ROMAN-STYLE SPRING VEGETABLES
Vignarola

This celebration of spring flavours appears in Tuscany and Lazio when the days get longer and warmer around April and May. It was traditionally eaten by workers in the vineyards as they pruned and managed the vines for the coming summer's growth of grapes. It is sometimes made with prosciutto, the wafer-thin slices pulled apart and folded in right at the end while the stew is resting, but I like the simplicity of this vegetable-only version and the fact that it's a great vegan dish. It should be eaten at room temperature with crusty bread.

For four:
1kg broad beans in their pods
1kg fresh peas in their pods
6 baby artichokes
juice of 1 lemon
300g chard, roughly chopped
extra virgin olive oil
4 bulbous spring onions, finely sliced
flaky sea salt
150ml white wine
a large handful of mint leaves, roughly chopped
black pepper

Pod the broad beans and peas. The kilogram of each should yield approximately 400g broad beans and 400g peas after deducting all the ones you've stolen to eat raw.

Trim the artichokes of their hard outer leaves and woody stem and remove and discard the hairy choke. Slice into quarters lengthways and immediately put into cold water with the lemon juice.

In a large pan of salted boiling water, blanch the broad beans for 2 minutes and remove with a slotted spoon. Now add the chard for a minute or two until it starts to wilt. Drain and set aside.

Heat 2 or 3 good glugs of olive oil in a very large saucepan. Soften the spring onions for 10 minutes until soft and glossy. Add the drained artichokes, mix, and continue to sauté gently for another 10 minutes. Then add the broad beans, the shelled peas and the chard. Stir again, adding a pinch or two of salt. Pour in the wine. Bring to the boil very briefly, then reduce to a simmer for 12 minutes or so, adding a splash of water if the liquid dries out. Stir in the mint. Taste and adjust the seasoning if necessary.

Remove from the heat and allow to rest for 30 minutes. Serve at room temperature with a twist of black pepper and a drizzle of olive oil.

ASPARAGUS & SAFFRON RISOTTO
Risotto con asparagi e zafferano

Chefs get quite excited in April when asparagus season begins, and with good reason. The fecund qualities of spring are perfectly encapsulated by these plump, green spears — they represent new life, growth, and are undeniably phallic to boot. Saffron is a historic Italian spice, used for centuries to show off and prove wealth — gram for gram it's more expensive than gold, after all. It appears most famously in the risotto that accompanies osso bucco in Lombardy but works a treat in this Florentine dish too.

For four:
1 litre vegetable stock (page 208)
extra virgin olive oil
1 large white onion, diced very finely
320g Carnaroli rice
flaky sea salt
200ml dry vermouth
12 asparagus spears, woody stems removed, sliced lengthways, then cut into
    2cm pieces
1 scant teaspoon saffron
80g unsalted butter
80g grated Parmesan, plus some extra for the table
black pepper

Heat the vegetable stock in a large pan on the back of the hob and keep it hot, bubbling very gently.

Pour 3 tablespoons of extra virgin olive oil into a large, heavy-based saucepan and place over a low to medium heat. Add the finely chopped onion and stir slowly for 10 minutes, making sure the onion does not brown. Reduce the heat or add more oil if necessary. Your onion should be glossy and translucent, never coloured.

Add the rice and make sure you coat every grain thoroughly. Add a large pinch of sea salt flakes. Turn the heat up and stir again. When the rice / onion mixture appears to be getting dry, throw in the vermouth. Favourite moment: that cloud of boozy steam. Keep stirring until all the vermouth has been absorbed, then add a ladleful of the hot stock and stir again.

Now, keep an eye on the clock. Over the next 20 minutes continue to add a little more stock every time the risotto appears to be absorbing the previous ladleful. At the 10-minute mark, stir in the asparagus and saffron, adding more stock with restraint. The trick is never to allow the mixture to become dry but also never to flood it either.

At the 20-minute mark, test the rice by biting it between your front teeth. It should yield and not be too firm. When you're happy it's done, turn up the heat, add the butter, and stir enthusiastically until it has melted. Remove the pan from the hob and allow the risotto to rest for a minute. Now gently stir in the grated Parmesan, serve on to four warmed plates, and offer extra Parmesan and a pepper grinder.

CANNELLINI BEAN
& CAVOLO NERO BROTH
Ribollita

When we first put ribollita on the menu at B R U T T O we used a version that included tinned chopped plum tomatoes. It's a perfectly legitimate iteration of a classic dish, but many Florentine friends were furious. 'No tomatoes,' they scolded. 'It's a bean broth, not a tomato soup.' I had to admit they were correct. Many Tuscan recipes include pancetta, but I prefer this vegetarian | vegan version.

Ribollita means 're-boiled', and like many soups and broths, it is better on the second day after it has had time to develop in flavour and texture. Just leave it overnight, covered and somewhere cool, and reheat the next day.

For four:
300g dried cannellini beans
1 whole head of cavolo nero
extra virgin olive oil
1 large onion, finely diced
1 large carrot, peeled and finely diced
1 celery stalk, finely diced
1 clove of garlic, finely chopped
flaky sea salt
1 teaspoon fennel seeds, crushed
a small handful of thyme leaves
black pepper
1 tablespoon tomato purée
1 large potato, peeled and diced
300ml vegetable stock (page 208)
1 bay leaf
½ a loaf of stale bread, crustless, torn into small chunks

Soak the beans overnight in plenty of cold water in a very large bowl.

The next day, when you're ready to start cooking, drain the beans and transfer them to a large pan. Cover them well with fresh cold water, bring to the boil, then reduce to a low simmer for 1 hour until soft. Remove the scum while cooking as it comes to the surface. Retain a cup of the cooking water, drain the beans and set them aside.

To prepare the head of cavolo nero, remove the base, then grab the thick ends of the stalks with one hand and gently pull the leaves away. Discard the stalks and base and roughly shred the leaves.

In a large, heavy-based saucepan, heat a good glug or two of olive oil and gently sauté the onion, carrot, celery and garlic for a good 15 minutes, until soft and glossy. Add a pinch or two of salt, the crushed fennel seeds, the thyme and a twist of black pepper. Stir in the tomato purée.

Now add the cooked beans, the diced potato, the stock and the bay leaf, and stir over a medium heat for about 45 minutes. Halfway through, add the chunks of stale bread and the shredded cavolo nero. Make sure the ingredients are submerged and always covered by liquid, stirring from time to time. Use the reserved bean cooking water if the broth is looking too dry.

Remove the bay leaf and taste, adjusting the seasoning as required. Serve in four warmed bowls with a twist of black pepper and a drizzle of olive oil. Or leave it overnight and reheat the next day, staying true to the name of the dish …

PENNE WITH VODKA & TOMATO SAUCE
Pasta alla vodka

I first had this dish at the cult restaurant Alla Vecchia Bettola (page 292) on a busy corner by a main road on the outskirts of Oltrarno in Florence. It's one of those slightly kitsch recipes that was popular in the 1980s and which has been enjoying something of a revival in Italy and even now in New York. Despite the potentially gimmicky nature of the addition of vodka, it works exceptionally well and is a favourite at BRUTTO. Most supermarket penne is rigate *— with ridges. If you can find penne* lisce *— smaller and without ridges — this makes a much more authentic version of this dish.*

For four:
2 × 400g tins of plum tomatoes
1 large onion, finely diced
extra virgin olive oil
flaky sea salt
1 clove of garlic, finely chopped
½ teaspoon chilli flakes
1 teaspoon dried oregano
200ml vodka
320g dried penne *lisce* (or penne *rigate* if you can't find the smooth variety)
4 tablespoons double cream
2 teaspoons caster sugar
100g grated Parmesan

Drain the tomatoes, reserving the juice for another purpose.

Place a large, ovenproof saucepan over a low to medium heat and gently sauté the onion in a couple of tablespoons of olive oil with a pinch of salt for 12–15 minutes until glossy and translucent, being careful not to let the onion brown. Add the garlic, chilli flakes and oregano and combine, stirring for a few more minutes. Pour in the vodka, increase the heat a little to bring to a very gentle bubble, and cook until the liquid has reduced by a third. Preheat the oven to 140°C.

Now add the drained tomatoes to the saucepan with a good pinch of salt and continue to gently boil for just 1 or 2 minutes, until the oven is ready. Transfer the saucepan to the oven, uncovered, and bake for 30–40 minutes, until the sauce has reduced and has coloured a little on top.

Meanwhile, cook the penne in plenty of salted boiling water. Drain the pasta. Remove the tomatoes from the oven, and add the double cream, sugar and half the Parmesan. Using a stick blender, create a smooth sauce. Immediately add the cooked penne and stir until fully combined. Adjust the seasoning if necessary and serve in four warmed bowls, with the remaining Parmesan on the table.

TOMATO & BREAD SOUP
Pappa al pomodoro

A gloriously authentic peasant staple and a wonderfully simple expression of Tuscan flavours. The tomatoes used for this dish are the very distinctive Florentine Costoluto variety, flat with ridges, that might be a challenge to find outside of Italy but by no means impossible. It's worth the extra effort to seek them out in well-stocked food halls and Italian delis. If not, those widely available big beef tomatoes would make a good substitute.

For four:
500g Florentine Costoluto tomatoes
flaky sea salt
750ml vegetable stock (page 208)
2 cloves of garlic, finely chopped
a large handful of basil leaves, roughly torn
350g stale sourdough, crusts removed
extra virgin olive oil
black pepper

De-stalk the tomatoes, cut them in half and deseed them. Discard the stalks and seeds. Roughly chop the tomato flesh into pieces the size of small dice and liberally sprinkle with salt. Leave for 30 minutes.

Meanwhile, pour the stock into a large saucepan and bring to the boil. Add the chopped tomatoes, the chopped garlic and half the torn basil. Boil for 2 minutes, then reduce to a simmer for 30 minutes, stirring occasionally.

Tear the stale sourdough into small pieces and add to the tomatoes and stock. Make sure the bread is submerged and continue to stir on a low heat for a further 20 minutes, or until the bread has absorbed the liquid and has started to look mushy. Cover and remove from the heat. Allow to rest for 15 minutes.

Taste the soup and adjust the seasoning if necessary. Serve in warmed bowls with a scattering of the remaining basil leaves, a drizzle of olive oil and a good twist or two of black pepper.

RISOTTO WITH MEAT SAUCE
Risotto con carne

I am used to delicate risotto dishes with vegetables or fish, a tradition I learnt when living in Venice and cooking exclusively from that region. So this recipe, a version of which I tried at Cibrèo (page 293) near Piazza dei Ciompi in Florence, was a very nice surprise. It is rich and unctuous, and I'd recommend a smaller portion than normal as a primo, but it is worth making and trying as a very authentic Tuscan iteration of the classic rice dish, perfect in winter months.

For four:
1 litre *brodo* (page 202), or beef stock
extra virgin olive oil
1 large onion, finely diced
flaky sea salt
1 small carrot, peeled and finely diced
1 celery stalk, finely diced
125g minced veal or pork, of a combination of both
1 chicken liver, cleaned and chopped
2 tablespoons tomato purée
100ml red wine
300g Carnaroli rice
a large knob of butter
100g grated Parmesan
black pepper

Bring the *brodo* to the boil in a large pan on the back of the hob, then reduce to a low simmer.

Heat a good glug of olive oil in another large saucepan and add half the chopped onion with a pinch of salt, and the carrot and celery. Gently sauté over a medium heat for 15 minutes, until soft and glossy. Add the minced meat and chopped chicken liver. Stir until the meat is brown, add the tomato purée and a cup of the *brodo*, and stir. Reduce a little, then add the red wine and simmer for about 10 minutes.

Meanwhile, in a third large saucepan, heat a glug of olive oil and sweat the remaining onion. When it is translucent and soft, after about 10 minutes, add the rice and stir, coating every grain. Introduce the *brodo*, a little ladleful at a time, over the following 15 minutes, never allowing the rice to dry out but never flooding it either.

Add the meat sauce to the pan of risotto, and continue to cook and stir for another 5 minutes or so, adding more *brodo* a little at a time as above. Test a grain of rice between your front teeth. It should yield easily but still have a little bite. When it tastes ready, add more salt if necessary, stir in the butter enthusiastically until it has melted completely, then take off the heat and gently fold in about two-thirds of the grated Parmesan. Serve while hot, with black pepper and the remaining Parmesan scattered over the top if you like.

BUCATINI WITH PECORINO, LEMON & BASIL

Bucatini con cacio, limone e basilico

Bucatini, one of my favourite pasta shapes, is thicker than spaghetti and has a miraculous hole that runs right through the middle of the long strands. It's got a very pleasing mouthfeel and holds sauce incredibly well. The zesty spring flavours of this recipe are so perfectly matched with salty Pecorino, known locally in Lazio and Tuscany as cacio, that it's a lovely alternative to the meatier dishes these regions are better known for. The principle of the sauce is close to carbonara, but without the need for pork cheek or pancetta. If you can get your hands on an Amalfi lemon, all the better, but a good, plump, unwaxed, common-or-garden lemon will do.

For four:
1 Amalfi lemon
150g grated Pecorino
2 medium free-range eggs
320g bucatini
extra virgin olive oil
a large handful of basil leaves, roughly torn
flaky sea salt
black pepper

Using a zester or a microplane or the fine side of a cheese-grater, remove as much zest as you can from the lemon. Set aside. Now juice half the lemon, making sure to remove and discard any pips. You only need about a tablespoon. Also set aside.

Put three-quarters of the grated Pecorino into a bowl and crack in the eggs. Whisk together thoroughly to create a smooth liquid paste. Set aside.

Cook the bucatini in plenty of salted boiling water according to the packet's instructions. When done – soft but still *al dente* – retain a small cup of the cooking water and drain the pasta.

Heat a few glugs of olive oil in a very large frying pan and transfer the drained pasta. Toss on a low heat with most of the torn basil and a pinch of salt for 1 minute. Add the egg and cheese mixture along with the lemon juice, stir thoroughly, and turn off the heat. Stir for another 30 seconds, adding a little of the retained pasta cooking water to loosen the mixture.

Serve on warmed plates with the remaining basil scattered over, the rest of the Pecorino equally distributed, the lemon zest, and a good twist of black pepper.

'NOT' FRENCH ONION SOUP
Zuppa di cipolle

One of my favourite books on Florentine cooking, La Cucina Fiorentina *by Aldo Santini, has a lot of information about the origins of some of the most traditional Tuscan dishes. It also makes some bold claims about other international recipes that Santini postulates originated in Florence and the surrounding areas. This includes his suggestion that French onion soup may actually be a Florentine dish, not a French one. 'La zuppa di cipolle è nostra e guai a chi ce la tocca.' (Onion soup is ours and woe betide anyone who touches it …) I love this. There's nothing like a bit of regional controversy to add flavour to an origin story.*

Many recipes place the bread at the bottom of the bowl before pouring in the soup, but I prefer to mimic the French (Florentine?) version with a large, cheesy crouton.

For four:
1.5 litres vegetable stock (page 208)
6 very large onions
2 red onions
extra virgin olive oil
a large knob of butter
flaky sea salt
black pepper
½ a small sourdough loaf
150g grated Parmesan

Heat the stock and keep it hot but not boiling on the back of the hob.

Peel the onions and slice them into thick rings. They may seem huge at this stage but they reduce dramatically in the cooking process. Heat a very good glug of olive oil with the butter in your largest saucepan and add the onions and a good pinch of salt. Stir to coat all the rings and sauté over a relatively high heat for about 5–8 minutes until they start to brown. Add a splash more oil if they start to stick to the pan.

When nicely browned, add a ladleful of stock and reduce the heat to a simmer. Cook for about 1 hour, adding more stock a little at a time when it looks as if it's drying out. Avoid the temptation to put all the stock in at once: the onions will develop in flavour if you take the softly-softly approach, even though all the stock should go in eventually over the hour. Check the seasoning and adjust if necessary. Cover and take off the heat. Allow to rest for 10 minutes.

Slice four 2cm pieces from the sourdough and lay them on a baking sheet. Distribute the grated Parmesan over the bread and place under a grill until melted, but not too brown.

Serve the onion soup in four wide, shallow bowls and lay a slice of the sourdough with melted Parmesan on top of each. Give each portion a good twist of black pepper.

CHILLI & GARLIC SPAGHETTI
Spaghetti aglio, olio e peperoncino

A very reliable and easy store-cupboard fall-back when you've not got any fresh ingredients in the fridge but need a tasty pasta dish and you're bored with the supermarket pesto from a jar you've had three times already since Monday. You can substitute the chilli flakes with real hot chillies if you have them, deseeded and finely chopped, but the below recipe is the classic pantry dish, so useful for emergencies and lazy days.

For four:
300g spaghetti
flaky sea salt
extra virgin olive oil
2 cloves of garlic, very finely chopped
2 heaped teaspoons chilli flakes
a small handful of flat parsley, chopped roughly (optional)

Bring a very large saucepan of salted water to the boil and cook the spaghetti according to the packet's instructions.

Meanwhile, in your largest frying pan, heat about 4 tablespoons of olive oil on a low to medium heat and gently sauté the chopped garlic and the chilli flakes. Do not allow the garlic to turn brown.

When the pasta is done, but still with a slight *al dente* bite, drain and transfer to the pan of oil and garlic, stirring thoroughly to combine all the ingredients and fully coat the spaghetti.

Scatter over the parsley (if using), and serve without Parmesan and, traditionally, without black pepper either.

SPINACH & RICOTTA DUMPLINGS
Gnudi

Gnudi *translates as 'naked', as these little dumplings are the most nude and simple form of homemade pasta you can make. The combination of spinach and ricotta is a very traditional marriage and appears in much of the pasta of the region, in ravioli and crespelle for example. It's a very satisfying process, and easy enough for children to help with in the kitchen if you want to encourage an early interest in Italian cooking for little chefs.*

For four:
500g baby spinach leaves, washed
50g '00' flour
250g ricotta
1 large free-range egg, beaten
150g grated Parmesan
flaky sea salt
black pepper
½ teaspoon freshly grated nutmeg
250g semolina
100g butter
a large handful of sage leaves

Steam the spinach for 3 minutes over a large pan of boiling water. Thoroughly drain and squeeze to remove the excess water, then chop the leaves finely. Set aside.

Mix the flour with the ricotta in a large bowl until it resembles lumpy breadcrumbs. Stir in the egg and two-thirds of the Parmesan. Add a pinch of salt, a twist of black pepper, the nutmeg and then add the spinach. Combine thoroughly with a wooden spoon or with your hands.

Put half the semolina into a bowl and shake the rest on to a baking sheet or a tray. Take small lumps of the flour, egg and spinach mixture and form them into small balls by rolling them between your palms, to the size of large olives. Turn each ball through the bowl of semolina, then place on the tray you've prepared with the rest of the semolina. When finished, you should have 24–30 little balls.

Fill a very large pan with water and bring to a rolling boil. Place the *gnudi* in the boiling water as quickly as possible, bringing it back to the boil on the highest heat, and continue to simmer for about 3 minutes.

Meanwhile, in a small saucepan over a medium heat, melt the butter and add the sage leaves. When it bubbles, reduce to a very low heat. This should take no more than 2 minutes, while the *gnudi* are cooking.

The *gnudi* will float to the surface when they are ready. Turn off the heat, remove them with a slotted spoon and drain the excess water on kitchen paper. Place on four warmed plates, pour the butter and sage over the top, then evenly distribute the remaining Parmesan. Add a flourish of black pepper.

PROSCIUTTO & MORTADELLA TORTELLONI IN CLEAR BROTH

Tortelloni in brodo

A classic from the Emilia-Romagna region of Italy but a firm favourite at Sostanza in Florence (page 303) and trattorie across many other regions too. In a casual poll of friends, chefs and Italophile food fans this dish came top of the list as an 'all-time favourite', and I have to say I don't disagree. It's much easier to get the correct thickness of the sheets using a pasta machine, but if you're a skilled enough baker used to making pastry for pies and tarts you should be able to achieve it with a rolling pin. We use brodo at BRUTTO, but good clear chicken stock could also be used and is just as delicious.

For four:

For the filling:
100g prosciutto, chopped
100g mortadella, chopped
80g grated Parmesan, and more for serving
a large knob of butter
1 medium free-range egg
½ teaspoon freshly grated nutmeg

For the pasta:
350g '00' flour, and more for dusting
2 large free-range eggs
3 free-range egg yolks

For the broth:
1 litre *brodo* (page 202), or chicken stock (page 205)

Start by placing all the filling ingredients in a food processor and creating a mince paste. (You could also do this manually in a bowl or a large pestle and mortar using lots of elbow grease.) When it's nicely smooth, set aside, covered.

To make the pasta, empty the flour on to a clean work surface and make a well in the middle, like a wide volcano. Put the eggs and yolks into the centre and carefully bring the sides in to create a dough. Knead until smooth and cut the ball in two. Wrap each in clingfilm and allow to rest for 45 minutes.

Keep one half wrapped while you work on the first half. Pass the dough through the pasta machine on the widest setting and repeat several times, folding it into three and turning it one quarter before feeding it through again. Make the dough progressively thinner by adjusting the setting down to a final 1mm. Lay the sheet on a floured work surface and, using a very sharp knife or roller cutter, cut it into 5cm squares. Cover with clingfilm to stop it drying too much, then do the same to the second half of the dough. You should end up with around 48 squares, maybe more.

Place a dollop of your mortadella and prosciutto minced paste in the centre of each square. Fold them in half, one by one, sealing the edges with a little pressure from your thumb and finger, to create filled triangles. Fold again to bring the tip of the triangle down to the base of the triangle. Now gently fold the long edges around a finger until the edges meet and you're left with a neat ring.

Heat the *brodo* in a very large saucepan. Test and adjust the seasoning if necessary. When it's boiling, put the tortelloni in. After about 2 minutes they will rise to the surface. As they do, remove them with a slotted spoon and distribute them evenly between four large warmed bowls. Ladle the *brodo* into each bowl. (Alternatively, I like to cook the tortelloni in a separate large pan of salted boiling water, drain them when ready, place them in the bowls and pour over the heated *brodo*. This ensures the *brodo* is nicely clear.)

Serve with roughly grated Parmesan – I like to use the scary side of the box grater with all the sharp holes.

FLORENTINE RAVIOLI
Ravioli alla fiorentina

Another example of spinach and ricotta coming together, confirming my hunch that it is Tuscany's favourite pairing. This is also the most typical ravioli I have found in Florence when eating out, and I'm told it's a very popular choice with home cooks, too. Ricotta is such a mild, young cheese that it lends delicacy here, resulting in a surprisingly light dish for a pasta course.

For four to six:

For the filling:
650g baby spinach, thoroughly washed
350g ricotta
1 large free-range egg
50g grated Parmesan, and more for serving
a few pinches of flaky sea salt
a twist or two of black pepper
½ teaspoon freshly grated nutmeg

For the pasta:
1 portion of simple pasta dough (page 222)

For the sauce:
150g butter
a handful of sage leaves, no stalks

Make the filling first. Cook the spinach in a large saucepan with a few splashes of water. It will wilt very quickly. When it's a dark green mush, drain and squeeze all the water out. Allow it to cool, then chop it finely. Put it into a large mixing bowl with the other filling ingredients and mix thoroughly until it's a lovely pale green paste. Set aside.

Roll out the pasta dough as per the instructions on page 93, using a pasta machine or a floured rolling pin. Lay the 1mm sheets on a floured surface and cut into 7cm squares. Place a large grape-sized dollop of the spinach mix on half the squares and lay another square on top of each. Use a little sprayed water if necessary to help seal them. Press the edges down gently to create 24–30 ravioli.

Bring a very large pan of salted water to the boil. Meanwhile, gently melt the butter in a large frying pan, add the sage leaves, let the butter bubble, then reduce to a very low heat. Put the ravioli into the boiling water. After about 4 minutes, remove with a slotted spoon on to a clean tea towel. Distribute equally on to warmed plates and pour over the melted butter and sage. Serve with the grated Parmesan.

PORK & SAGE RAVIOLI
Ravioli di maiale e salvia

The Central Market in Florence is best known for its massive T-bone steaks and offal, but outdoor-reared pork features on most stalls and is easy to get outside Italy at even the most humble butcher in the towns and provinces of the UK, Europe and the United States. I must insist that you buy high-welfare minced pork, since the intensively farmed factory pork in cheap supermarkets encourages heinous practices and is also rather insipid and tasteless.

For four:

For the filling:
extra virgin olive oil
1 small onion, finely chopped
1 small carrot, peeled and finely chopped
½ celery stalk, finely chopped
flaky sea salt
1 clove of garlic, very finely chopped
300g high-welfare, outdoor-reared pork mince
a small handful of sage leaves, chopped
½ teaspoon freshly grated nutmeg

For the pasta:
350g '00' flour
2 large free-range eggs
3 free-range egg yolks

To serve:
150g butter
black pepper
80g grated Parmesan

In a large, heavy-bottomed saucepan, heat a few glugs of olive oil over a low to medium heat and soften the onion, carrot and celery for 12 minutes, adding a large pinch of salt. Make sure nothing browns. Add the garlic and continue to sauté for another 2 minutes. Now add the pork mince, chopped sage and nutmeg and continue for another 4–5 minutes until the pork is browned slightly. Transfer to a food blender and purée until smooth, adding a little olive oil if necessary. Set aside.

Make the pasta dough exactly as per pages 92–3, then roll, cover, and cut into 7cm squares. Place dollops of the pork mix in the centre of half the squares and follow the same procedure as per the previous recipe (page 95).

Cook the ravioli in plenty of salted boiling water for 4 minutes while melting the butter in a large frying pan. Don't let it burn. Distribute the ravioli on to four warmed plates, pour over the melted butter, garnish with lots of black pepper and the Parmesan, and serve.

POLENTA WITH CANNELLINI BEANS, CHARD & PANCETTA
Farinata

This is another of those revelations: a dish that I hadn't tried before I started researching Tuscan food. It's a wonderfully comforting combination of textures and flavours. When I'm in Italy I'll often get a sudden pang for polenta — I can't explain why. It happened on a research trip a few years ago when I was lucky enough to have a small rented apartment with a tiny two-ring electric stove. I made the recipe below and I'm afraid, dear reader, I ate the lot.

For four:
700ml vegetable stock (page 208)
a large bunch of Swiss chard, washed
extra virgin olive oil
1 onion, finely diced
1 carrot, peeled and finely diced
1 celery stalk, finely diced
flaky sea salt
1 clove of garlic, very finely sliced
50g unsmoked pancetta, cut into small cubes or small matchsticks
2 tablespoons tomato purée
275g cooked cannellini beans (page 76)
200g polenta
black pepper

Heat the stock in a saucepan and leave simmering on the back of the hob.

Cut the large stems from the chard and discard. Roughly chop the leaves. Set aside.

Pour a good amount of olive oil into a separate saucepan, preferably your largest, and place on a low to medium heat. Sauté the onion, carrot and celery with a good pinch of salt for 12 minutes until glossy and translucent, but don't let it burn. Add the garlic and the pancetta and stir for another 3 minutes. Now stir in the chopped chard and the tomato purée. When everything is combined and coated, pour in the hot stock. Bring to the boil, then reduce to a simmer for 15 minutes.

Add the cooked cannellini beans and top up with boiled water from the kettle at this stage if it's looking too dry. Stir, then slowly introduce the polenta. Continue to simmer on a low heat for another 20–25 minutes. During this time, test and adjust the seasoning.

Serve in warmed bowls, with a very generous drizzle of good olive oil and a twist of black pepper.

EGG MACARONI WITH ASPARAGUS, PEAS & COURGETTES

Maccheroni all'uovo con verdure di stagione

Quite soon after BRUTTO opened we received a few requests from our customers for dishes that weren't as meat-heavy as the majority of traditional Florentine fare. It was a fair point. As our opening months were across winter, we introduced pasta e fagioli and ribollita, both hearty celebrations of vegetables that were available in the colder seasons. But as soon as spring arrived we turned to the green bounty of that season and put this dish on the menu. It was an instant hit. The recipe uses Parmesan, which contains rennet and isn't suitable for true vegetarians, so please substitute it with one of the many Parmesan-style rennet-free alternatives.

For four:
12 asparagus spears
2 courgettes
500g fresh peas (to yield 200g when podded)
a small handful of fresh mint leaves
a small handful of flat parsley leaves
extra virgin olive oil
flaky sea salt
320g large fresh macaroni
a knob of butter
80g grated Parmesan (or vegetarian alternative)
black pepper

Cut and discard the woody stalks from the asparagus and slice the stalks thinly at an angle. Top and tail the courgettes and cut down the middle lengthways, then slice thinly. Pod the peas. Shred the mint and parsley very finely with a sharp knife.

Place a large saucepan of salted water on a high heat and bring to the boil. Pour a few glugs of olive oil into a large, wide pan on a medium heat and gently sauté the asparagus, courgettes and peas with a pinch of salt for about 10 minutes, until soft but not browned.

Put the fresh macaroni into the boiling water and cook for 4 minutes until *al dente* – still with a slight bite. Retaining a cup of the cooking water, drain the pasta and add it to the large pan of vegetables. Turn up the heat, add the butter, half the grated cheese and the herbs and stir for 1 minute, using a little of the pasta water to loosen the mixture.

Serve on four warmed plates and scatter over the remaining grated cheese with a twist of black pepper.

CHICKPEA SOUP
Zuppa di ceci

Sometimes called carne dei poveri — *'paupers' meat' — chickpeas are a very common Tuscan ingredient, popular because they're inexpensive but also a great source of protein. This hearty soup could easily satisfy as a single-course lunch with a hunk of crusty bread, or in more modest quantities for a tasty first course.*

For four:
extra virgin olive oil
1 large onion, sliced
1 large carrot, peeled and diced
1 celery stalk, thinly sliced
1 clove of garlic, finely sliced
a handful of rosemary leaves, no stalks
3 tablespoons tomato purée
400g dried chickpeas, soaked in cold water overnight
flaky sea salt
black pepper

In a very large saucepan, heat a good glug of olive oil on a low heat and very gently sauté the onion, carrot and celery for 10 minutes until the onion is glossy and translucent. Add the garlic and rosemary and stir for a few minutes more, still on a low heat, making sure nothing browns. Add the tomato purée and stir. It's important not to add salt at this stage, even if you're tempted.

Drain the chickpeas and transfer them to the saucepan. Stir to coat them with the gently sautéd ingredients, then add 1 litre of cold water and turn the heat up fully. Bring to the boil, then reduce to a medium simmer for around 1 hour, unlidded. Keep an eye on the pan to remove any scum from the surface and to top up with hot water as necessary. After an hour, test a chickpea to see if it's tender. If not, continue for another 15–20 minutes until soft.

Remove just over half the contents and purée them in a blender. When smooth, return the mixture to the pan and add a good pinch of salt and a twist of black pepper or two. Taste and adjust if necessary.

Ladle into warmed bowls and drizzle a very decent amount of olive oil on to the surface of each serving. You really must be able to see the oil glisten. Serve with crusty bread.

RIGATONI WITH WILD BOAR & CHIANTI

Rigatoni con cinghale e Chianti

Wild boar are ubiquitous in Tuscany. You see them running around all over the place in rural areas, I even sometimes come across them as roadkill when driving around the hills outside Siena and Florence. It's not so easy to find them in other parts of Europe and in the United States. However, good Italian delis will usually stock imported wild boar sausages. It's the meat inside the sausage skins we are after here, and the funky flavour is a true taste of Tuscany.

For four:
extra virgin olive oil
1 large onion, thinly sliced
flaky sea salt
1 clove of garlic, very finely sliced
4 plump wild boar sausages
a handful of thyme leaves, chopped
a handful of sage leaves, chopped
2 tablespoons tomato purée
black pepper
100ml Chianti
320g rigatoni
80g grated Parmesan, and more for serving

Pour a couple of tablespoons of olive oil into a large, heavy-bottomed saucepan and sauté the sliced onions with a pinch of salt on a low to medium heat until soft and glossy – about 12–15 minutes. Add the garlic towards the end but make sure nothing browns. Meanwhile, remove the skins from the sausages and crumble the meat. Discard the skins.

Add the crumbled sausage meat to the onions with the chopped herbs, then turn up the heat a little, stir and cook until the meat browns slightly. Add the tomato purée and a twist of pepper and stir. Pour in the Chianti and let it bubble gently until reduced by half – about 10 minutes.

Meanwhile, heat a very large pan of salted water and when boiling, add the pasta and cook according to the packet's instructions minus 1 minute. Drain the rigatoni, reserving a small cup of the cooking water. Add the drained pasta to the sausage mixture and combine fully, using the retained pasta water if the sauce needs loosening, stirring for a minute or so. Take off the heat, fold in the Parmesan, and serve on warmed plates with a drizzle of olive oil, a twist of pepper, and more Parmesan if you like.

EGGS FLORENTINE
Uova alla fiorentina

I include this recipe with my tongue firmly in my cheek. It's not Florentine at all, of course, but the rest of the world might assume it is. The back-story is much more interesting than the dish. Catherine de' Medici, the daughter of Florence's ruler Lorenzo II, married Henry II of France in 1533 and took her servants and chefs to Paris. She was a lover of spinach, found all around Florence in abundance, and insisted on it with every meal. She even took it with her to grow in France. Subsequently, any dish with spinach was, at the time, given the descriptor 'Florentine' in honour of the queen.

For four:
4 medium free-range eggs
2 English muffins
butter, for spreading
400g baby spinach leaves, thoroughly washed
flaky sea salt
nutmeg
black pepper

For the hollandaise sauce:
2 large free-range egg yolks
salt
white wine vinegar
100g butter
2 tablespoons lemon juice

You will need four saucepans.

Start by making the hollandaise sauce. Take a heatproof glass bowl that will fit over a saucepan, half-fill that pan with water and bring it to the boil. Put the egg yolks into the glass bowl with a pinch of salt and a mere splash of white wine vinegar. Whisk thoroughly, adding a tablespoon of cold water, then set the bowl aside for a moment.

Take a separate saucepan, place over a low heat, and melt the butter. Reduce the pan of boiling water to a simmer.

Put the glass bowl over the gently simmering water and very slowly pour in the melted butter in a very thin stream to combine with the egg yolks, while stirring slowly to create a smooth sauce. Add a little more cold water if the sauce thickens too much. Finally, stir in the lemon juice and set aside covered, somewhere warm.

Boil water in a third and fourth saucepan (use a kettle if faster) and carefully crack the eggs into small teacups. Reduce the water in both pans to a simmer. Carefully lower the eggs into the first pan, one at a time. Poach the eggs for 3 minutes until cooked but still with a wobble. You want the yolks inside to be very soft still. Transfer to kitchen paper with a slotted spoon.

Split the muffins in half and toast them while the eggs are poaching. Butter lightly and place each half on a warmed plate. Put the spinach into the fourth pan and cook for 2 minutes, until the spinach has collapsed and significantly reduced in volume. Drain thoroughly, squeezing out all the water.

Divide the wilted spinach between the muffins, adding a pinch of salt. Place a poached egg on top of the spinach and pour over the hollandaise sauce. Add a small grating of nutmeg, a twist of black pepper, and serve immediately.

INSA

There is no section of the traditional *trattoria* menu that is simpler. Salads in Tuscany and in most other regions are usually a presentation of a single fresh ingredient – tomatoes, lettuce, radicchio – served with a dressing or often just with extra virgin olive oil and lemon juice. The philosophy, I suppose, is that nature has already done the hard work, so why would you interfere with what is already perfect by over-complicating?

That is not to say that there are no innovative and artful variations on a theme. Puntarelle, for example, is enhanced immeasurably by careful cutting, chilling, and the addition of the classic Roman dressing of garlic, anchovy and lemon juice. The result is so satisfying that home cooks and chefs in the regions of Lazio, Tuscany and beyond have been preparing the dish for centuries in this manner. The point is, this is the *only way* to eat puntarelle and I challenge anyone who says otherwise. Tradition is extremely important, even when presenting a single ingredient and not messing around with it.

In Tuscany, the persistence of *cucina povera* informs many of the classic salads. This is most noticeable in *panzanella*, where necessity proved to be the mother of invention: how do you deal with a glut of fresh tomatoes and an abundance of stale bread? Well, you combine them in the most economical way, wasting nothing, and simply adding a little acidity to create the most famous salad in the region.

A word on presentation: the salads in this section are all recipes for four people, but in my experience, putting the full four portions on to a single platter with serving spoons or into a large bowl with olivewood salad tossers at the centre of the table is much more fun and makes a meal into a convivial feast.

LATE

TUSCAN BREAD
& TOMATO SALAD
Panzanella

The first thing you will notice is that this doesn't look like the panzanella *salads you may have seen in other recipe books or in restaurants outside of Tuscany. I make no apologies — this is the authentic presentation. You'll have seen versions with big chunks of tomato, sliced red onion and croutons. Tasty, no doubt, but not a real* panzanella, *in my opinion.*

I first had the traditional version in a trattoria in Sovicille just outside Siena and then started to see it in other restaurants I visited. The texture resembles couscous, if anything, and the tomatoes are chopped finely to incorporate more easily with the soaked and crumbled bread.

For four:
½ a sourdough loaf, stale if possible (or use homemade Tuscan bread – page 226)
4 large Florentine Costoluto tomatoes, the ribbed ones
1 red onion, very finely diced
a handful of basil leaves, roughly torn
flaky sea salt
red wine vinegar
extra virgin olive oil
black pepper

Remove the crusts from the bread and discard. Cut the loaf into rough cubes and leave on a tray somewhere warm overnight to dry out. Alternatively, place in a preheated oven at 120°C for 10 minutes, being careful not to toast them. Place in a bowl, cover with cold water and leave for 10 minutes.

Destalk the tomatoes and remove the seeds. Chop very finely and place in a large serving bowl with the finely chopped red onion and half the torn basil. Scatter lightly with sea salt, stir several times and leave to rest for 10 minutes.

Meanwhile, drain the bread and squeeze out all the water with your hands. Crumble the bread in with the tomatoes and stir thoroughly, adding a splash of red wine vinegar and a good glug or two of olive oil. When everything is fully incorporated, place on the table with serving spoons and scatter over the remaining torn basil leaves. A little drizzle more of olive oil and a twist of black pepper at the table wouldn't hurt.

PUNTARELLE WITH ANCHOVY DRESSING
Puntarelle alla romana

I always get excited when I see this wonderful, bitter winter vegetable on market stalls in the colder months. Although it's sometimes called 'asparagus chicory', the etymology is false: it's just the inner spears that resemble asparagus. It's firmly in Camp Chicory.

Cutting the crunchy core into the right shapes can be a bit tricky, but will be made a whole lot easier if you can get your hands on the correct tool. It's a wooden frame with a lattice of tightly stretched wire resembling a small harp or tennis racquet. A quick search online for 'puntarelle cutter' will give you plenty of options to buy one for not very much money.

For four:
lots of ice cubes
1 large head of puntarelle, or 2 medium heads
1 × 50g tin of anchovies
½ a clove of garlic, chopped
juice of ½ a lemon
extra virgin olive oil
black pepper (optional)

Fill a large mixing bowl with cold water and add lots of ice cubes.

Strip off the outer leaves of the puntarelle and discard any that look brown. Do the same with the smaller inner leaves. Lay all the good leaves flat on a chopping board. Inside the puntarelle you will find a cluster of what look like short asparagus spears. Remove these from the solid, woody base and discard the base.

Put the smallest of the inner leaves into the iced water. Strip the green from the larger leaves and discard. Now, with a very sharp knife, slice all the white stalks lengthways. Then, if necessary, cut across the longer stalks to create 5–7cm sections. Plunge them into the ice bath.

Finally, push the asparagussy spears through your puntarelle cutter (or slice them thinly into matchstick shapes, lengthways) and add them to the iced water. Leave for 1 hour. They will curl and twist into gorgeous shapes.

Put the anchovies, including the oil from the tin, into a large pestle and mortar with the garlic. Mash together thoroughly until you have a paste. Transfer to a large serving bowl and loosen the paste with the lemon juice. Stir and add olive oil a little at a time while stirring to create a dressing.

Drain the puntarelle thoroughly and add to the serving bowl with the anchovy dressing. Incorporate fully with your hands and serve with salad tossers and a pepper grinder for an optional twist.

TUNA, WHITE BEAN & SHALLOT SALAD
Insalata di tonno, cannellini e cipolle

I'm very fond of dishes that can still be made using tinned versions of authentic ingredients. These are easy to store in the pantry for those occasions when you don't have time to prepare in advance or go shopping. This salad is typically Tuscan and is served frequently by home cooks as a convenient lunch. If you spend a little more on an excellent-quality tinned tuna it will make the salad all the better. I particularly like white tuna, which comes in jars and is satisfyingly chunky.

For four:
2 × 400g tins of cannellini beans, drained and rinsed
extra virgin olive oil
red wine vinegar
2 shallots, very finely sliced
flaky sea salt
black pepper
a handful of flat parsley leaves, chopped
2 × 112g tins of tuna

Place the drained and rinsed cannellini beans into a large mixing bowl and add a few glugs of olive oil and a good splash of red wine vinegar. Add one of the finely sliced shallots, a couple of pinches of salt and a twist or two of black pepper. Stir to incorporate. Add the chopped parsley and stir several times again. Leave for 5 minutes.

Open the tins of tuna and drain away any liquid. Evenly share the cannellini mix between four wide bowls. Carefully remove the chunks of tuna and distribute over each bowl, being careful to keep the flesh as intact as possible. Scatter over the remaining slices of shallot evenly and finish with a delicate drizzle of olive oil.

BROAD BEAN SALAD WITH PECORINO

Insalata di fave con Pecorino

'To pod, or not to pod. That is the question.'
Broad beans are easy to grow if you have the space in your garden for a vegetable patch. I was fortunate enough to have a few metres of good soil when I lived in Kent, fertilised for many years with manure from the previous owner's pet donkey. Every late spring I got an amazing crop of broad beans and ate this salad almost daily. If the broad beans are small, you won't need to double-pod. If they are big, you should. Double-podding reveals the bright green inner bean, which I think I prefer. It also makes the salad so much prettier.

For four:
2kg broad beans (to yield 800g when podded)
extra virgin olive oil
1 tablespoon lemon juice
flaky sea salt
60g Pecorino
2 teaspoons lemon zest
black pepper

Pull apart the pods and remove all the beans. Place a large saucepan on a high heat and bring to a vigorous boil. Put the beans into the pan and boil for 2 minutes at full throttle, but no more. Immediately drain and rinse the beans in cold water or under a running cold tap.

Take each bean, cut the skin at one end with your thumbnail, and push the shiny green inner bean out into a clean bowl. Discard the pale green skins.

Dress the beans with a good few glugs of olive oil, the lemon juice and a few pinches of sea salt. Mix together with a wooden spoon.

Using a potato peeler, shave the Pecorino into flakes.

Stir the beans again and distribute between four wide bowls. Scatter the shaved Pecorino over the top, drizzle a little more olive oil and finish with a scattering of lemon zest and a twist of black pepper.

A princely salad for a midsummer's day. (Full marks if you get this double Shakespeare reference from the introduction.)

BRUTTO GREEN SALAD
Insalata della casa

My original idea for our house salad was to dress and serve it tableside. I wanted the salad not just to taste like it had been made to order, but to show it actually being created in front of our customers. Often at BRUTTO the restaurant is just too full to bring out the serving table and perform the tossing and dressing. There's just no space. But I would suggest you do this at home in front of your family or guests, if nothing other than to add a bit of theatre to mealtimes and dinner parties.

For four:
1 large head of romaine lettuce (or 2 butterleaf lettuces)
2 celery stalks
1 large cucumber
3 tablespoons extra virgin olive oil
1 tablespoon red wine vinegar
2 teaspoons Dijon mustard
2 teaspoons dried tarragon
flaky sea salt
black pepper
caster sugar

Remove the base of the romaine or butterleaf lettuces and discard. Roughly shred into generous bite-sized pieces. Wash thoroughly and use a salad spinner to remove all water. Place in your largest serving bowl.

Peel the celery. It's an odd instruction, I know, but it does make for a better result. Then slice it very finely. Peel the cucumber, slice it lengthways, and remove the seeds by making a long triangular gulley. Finely slice the cucumber too. Add the celery and cucumber to the lettuce in the large bowl.

Take a clean jam jar with a tight-fitting lid and put in the olive oil, vinegar, mustard, tarragon, a good pinch of salt, a good twist of pepper and a couple of pinches of caster sugar. Shake vigorously until combined and emulsified.

Pour half the dressing into the prepared lettuce and toss several times. Taste a leaf to see whether you like it like that. I prefer my salads very lightly dressed but you might like more, in which case adjust to your preference. Place the bowl in the middle of the table, with two large olivewood salad tossers. Make sure everyone gets their fair share of cucumber and celery when you serve.

BITTER LEAVES WITH LEMON & PARSLEY

Radicchio tardivo con limone e prezzemolo

When in season, usually November to March, radicchio tardivo, the most noble and beautiful of the royal family of bitter chicories, is the one that draws your eye at market stalls and grocery shops. It has a very distinctive purple hue and tentacle-like fronds that start out white at the base and darken dramatically at the tips. It's a great ingredient in risotto and pasta, or simply roasted, but my favourite iteration is raw with good olive oil and the acid zing of lemon juice.

For four:
2 heads of radicchio Treviso tardivo
flaky sea salt
excellent extra virgin olive oil
zest and juice of 1 lemon
a handful of flat parsley leaves, finely chopped

Remove and discard the base of each head of tardivo. Cut crossways into 5cm pieces. Rinse in cold water and dry thoroughly in a salad spinner.

Place the radicchio in a large bowl with a couple of pinches of salt and a good glug or two of olive oil. Gently mix everything together with a wooden spoon. Add the lemon juice and chopped parsley and mix again. Evenly distribute between four wide plates with a scattering of lemon zest on each, or serve in the large bowl at the centre of the table with the zest tossed on top from a height. A large pair of salad tossers is essential so that everyone can help themselves if you decide to take the communal approach.

FLORENTINE TOMATO SALAD
Insalata di pomodoro Costoluto

When it comes to simplicity, Trattoria Sostanza in Florence (page 303) gets it right. I always think of Carly Simon's 'Nobody Does It Better'. When I first ordered their tomato salad I was delighted to see that it consisted of a large plate with two thick slices of ripe Costoluto tomatoes, oil, salt and nothing else.

Costoluto tomatoes are the flat, ribbed ones that are so closely associated with Florence that most people call them Florentine tomatoes. They must be ripe. They must be at room temperature. Never straight from the fridge. You could, I suppose, use ripe, organic beef tomatoes if you can't find the ribbed ones, but I would urge you to try harder.

For four:
4 Costoluto tomatoes
flaky sea salt
excellent extra virgin olive oil
black pepper (optional)
basil leaves (optional)

Take each tomato and slice off the stalk end and the bottom with a very sharp knife. Discard the ends.

Try to yield 8 or 12 slices from the 4 tomatoes. Arrange them evenly on four wide plates so that the slabs of tomato flesh overlap just slightly. Scatter over sea salt flakes as you crunch them between your thumb and fingers. Then, just after serving, drizzle your best olive oil, sparingly, on to each plate in front of your guests. I don't think this dish needs pepper, but you could have a peppermill to hand just in case. Garnish with a few torn basil leaves, if you like, but they're not essential.

CUCUMBER, MINT & CELERY LEAVES

Cetriolo, menta e foglie di sedano

It's a common complaint of mine, to anyone who will listen, that most supermarkets trim all the wonderful leaves from their celery before hermetically sealing them in plastic bags and piling them on to the shelves looking like decapitated versions of their former selves. Please try to find organic celery from an enlightened grocer, with all the frondy leaves intact. You won't need the stalks for this recipe, just the leaves.

For four:
4 small cucumbers
leaves from 1 head of celery
a large handful of mint leaves
flaky sea salt
extra virgin olive oil
juice of ½ a lemon

Cut the ends off the cucumbers and discard. Peel them but leave some of the skin, roughly half-and-half. Cut them lengthways and remove the seeds by scooping them out with a teaspoon. Discard the seeds. Cut horizontally into 1cm slices. Roughly chop some of the celery leaves but leave the smaller ones intact, and shred the mint leaves by piling them and slicing through to create thin, short ribbons.

Place everything in a large mixing bowl, crunch in a few pinches of sea salt and pour over a couple of glugs of olive oil. Stir, add the lemon juice, stir again for a minute, then transfer to a pretty serving dish or bowl with wooden serving spoons.

RAW YOUNG ARTICHOKES WITH BLACK OLIVES & PECORINO

Castraure, olive nere e Pecorino

Artichokes come in all shapes and sizes. The classic globe artichoke, steamed and served (in French cuisine) with a mustardy vinaigrette into which you dip the leaves and scrape the flesh off with your bottom teeth just won't do here. You need the smallest, youngest variety, known in Italy as castraure or botoli. These are the very delicate, often purple, buds that can be eaten raw once the harsh, tough outer leaves are removed. You'll find them outside Italy normally referred to as baby artichokes.

For four:
1 tablespoon lemon juice
12 baby artichokes
20 Taggiasca olives, pitted
80g Pecorino Romano
a large handful of flat parsley leaves
extra virgin olive oil
flaky sea salt
black pepper

Fill a large bowl with cold water and add the lemon juice. This is your acidulated water.

Remove and discard all the hard, outer leaves from the artichokes. There must be nothing left that is spiky or tough. Remove and discard all the hard stalk. Finely slice the remaining, soft artichoke core and immediately plunge the slices into the acidulated water.

Slice the Taggiasca olives finely and set aside. Shave the Pecorino with a potato peeler and set the flakes aside. Make sure the flat parsley leaves have no stalks. If the leaves are huge, slice them in half.

Drain the artichoke slices thoroughly and transfer them to a large serving bowl. Add the olives and the parsley with a couple of glugs of olive oil and stir well. Give the mix a pinch of salt and a twist of black pepper and stir again.

Transfer to four plates and evenly distribute the shaved Pecorino flakes.

ROMAN GRAIN SALAD
Insalata di farro

Farro is a wonderfully versatile grain that dates back approximately 20,000 years, to Mesopotamia. It's nutritious, tasty and makes a perfect ingredient in salads. It was an essential element of Roman soldiers' mealtimes and still persists in the regions around Lazio, including Tuscany. To keep the salad regional, I've used ricotta, which, like most cheese in Tuscany, is made from sheep's milk and has a lovely mild salty tang. But you could easily substitute mozzarella if you like.

For four:
250g farro
flaky sea salt
1 large courgette
1 large Costoluto tomato
1 red onion, very finely sliced
a large handful of basil leaves, roughly torn
extra virgin olive oil
red wine vinegar
150g fresh ricotta
black pepper

Place a large saucepan half-full of water on a high heat and bring to the boil. Add the farro with a pinch of salt and cook according to the packet's instructions, usually about 30 minutes. Drain and set aside to cool.

Meanwhile, top and tail the courgette and slice extremely thinly with a mandoline. The slices should be so thin that they are floppy rather than stiff.

De-stalk the tomato, cut in half down the middle, remove the seeds and chop into small pieces.

Combine the cooled farro with the tomato, courgette, red onion and basil leaves, add a good pinch of salt, a few glugs of olive oil and a splash of red wine vinegar. Stir several times and make sure everything is fully incorporated. Divide between four wide bowls, crumble over the moist ricotta and finish with a small drizzle of olive oil and a twist of black pepper.

POTATO, PEA & SPRING ONION SALAD
Insalata di patate, piselli e cipolline

Once again, this salad is all about getting the right ingredients. The potatoes must be waxy varieties such as Ratte, Charlotte or Jersey Royals. The spring onions must be the bulbous continental type, not the thin, chive-like supermarket versions. And the peas must be freshly podded. I'd also suggest making the dressing in advance in order to allow the flavours to develop, but remember to remove it from the fridge half an hour before you need to use it.

For four:
4 waxy potatoes, peeled
1kg peas in their pods (to yield 400g when podded)
4 bulbous spring onions
a handful of mint leaves, roughly sliced
zest of 1 lemon
flaky sea salt
black pepper

For the dressing:
1 heaped teaspoon capers
4 tablespoons extra virgin olive oil
1 tablespoon lemon juice
1 heaped teaspoon Dijon mustard
1 teaspoon dried parsley
a pinch of sea salt
a pinch of caster sugar

To make the dressing, mash the capers in a pestle and mortar to create a paste. Transfer to a clean jam jar with a tight-fitting lid and add the other dressing ingredients. Close the lid and shake vigorously until it has combined and emulsified.

Cook the peeled potatoes in boiling water for 15–20 minutes, until they yield when pierced with the tip of a sharp knife. Drain and rinse under cold water. Set aside.

Pod the peas and place in a large mixing bowl. Slice the white parts of the spring onions very finely and add to the bowl along with a few slices of the green upper parts and the chopped mint. Slice the cooled potatoes and add those too, with around half the dressing. Combine everything by mixing very gently with wooden salad tossers. Only add more dressing if you think it needs it – I prefer a light dressing for this salad, not too gloopy. Distribute between four wide plates or bowls and scatter over the lemon zest with a scant pinch of salt and a brief twist of black pepper.

CASTELFRANCO & PINK BITTER LEAF SALAD WITH AGED PARMESAN

Insalata di Castelfranco e radicchio rosa con Parmigiano

When I think of the various types of radicchio I am reminded of those charts which rank chillies in order of heat. In my mind, at the top of the radicchio chart is Treviso tardivo, the bitterest in the hierarchy. At the bottom is Castelfranco, the mildest. It's a delicately flavoured leaf with just a hint of the magic tang of radicchio. It's also very pretty, its striations of buttery yellow and pink making beautiful patterns on the plate. I've said this before, but I wonder if the fashion house Missoni took inspiration for its fabrics from this gorgeous lettuce.

By the way, please buy the most expensive aged Parmesan you can find. Five-year aged should suit nicely.

For four:
2 heads of Castelfranco
1 head of pink radicchio
3 tablespoons extra virgin olive oil, and more for serving
1 tablespoon lemon juice
flaky sea salt
black pepper
80g five-year aged Parmesan

Remove and discard the stems from the Castelfranco and the pink radicchio. Wash the leaves in a large basin of cold water and thoroughly drain. Use a salad spinner to remove the last of the water. Keep the leaves intact but if they are really large, slice them in half.

Place them in a very large mixing bowl and add the oil, lemon juice, a good pinch or two of salt and a generous twist of black pepper. Very gently turn over with your hands. Leave to stand while you shave flakes from the aged Parmesan using a potato peeler.

Evenly distribute the dressed leaves between four plates, scatter over the shavings of Parmesan and add a little slick of olive oil just before serving.

SEC

Florence is an unapologetically meaty city. Its restaurants and *trattorie* follow the traditions of the region in their menus and offer dishes that favour the flesh and eschew the fish. This can be frustrating to those who have decided to eat less or no meat for environmental, political or ethical reasons. For us at BRUTTO, running a restaurant in a multicultural city like London, we are frequently challenged by people asking why there aren't more vegetarian and pescatarian options. We always point back to our Florentine roots and inspiration.

Some of the very traditional, historical dishes are a bit too hardcore even for me, however. The famous *cibrèo*, for example, uses the floppy red bits from on top and underneath the male chicken's head – the cockscomb and the wattle – and at BRUTTO I decided that might be a little too challenging for the majority of our guests.

We have also developed dishes that recognise the current desire for lighter options and I looked back at the historical canon to find Tuscan traditions that focus on vegetables, fowl and fish. So there should be something for everyone in this section.

Needless to say, I urge you to always seek out butchers and fishmongers who practise enlightened policies of only stocking high-welfare, organic, free-range and sustainable produce.

BEEF SHIN & PEPPERCORN STEW
Peposo

The classic Florentine beef stew. It's a dish of extremely deep flavours and comforting textures. But it's not a preparation that can be rushed. You need at least four hours, preferably more, and as with many Tuscan recipes, it is improved by leaving overnight. I'd love to be able to say you can use an alternative cut if you can't get hold of beef shin, but it really must be shin. And you must leave the fat on – do not be tempted to trim. Your butcher will always be able to provide shin even if your supermarket can't.

Additionally, the wine element needs to be on-brand and regional. Chianti or even a standard Sangiovese will provide much better results than a cheap New World Merlot from a petrol station.

For four:
100g lard (or butter if you're afraid of lard)
800g beef shin, cut into small chunks
flaky sea salt
1 bottle Chianti or Sangiovese
2 cloves of garlic, finely sliced
2 tablespoons black peppercorns
2 × 400g tins of chopped tomatoes
black pepper
sourdough bread, for serving

Melt half the lard in a very large frying pan and sear the meat on all sides until nicely browned. Add a few pinches of salt during this process. You may need to fry in batches to avoid overcrowding the pan. If there is a dark residue at the bottom of the frying pan, deglaze with a splash of red wine. When all the shin is brown, transfer to a very large saucepan in which you have melted the remaining lard. Add the sliced garlic and the peppercorns and stir for 1 minute. Now add the chopped tomatoes and the rest of the wine. Bring to the boil briefly, then reduce to a very low simmer.

For the next 4 hours, keep half an eye on your *peposo* to make sure it's not drying out too quickly. If it is, cover it, but the full bottle of wine should have been sufficient to keep it stew-like. After 4 hours, check the seasoning and adjust if necessary. The beef shin will have disintegrated somewhat and become stringy and soft. You can encourage this further with some hearty wooden spoon action. If it hasn't, leave it longer. Or you could let it cool and leave it covered overnight. Then give it another 30 minutes on a medium heat the next day.

Serve with hunks of sourdough or unsalted Tuscan bread (page 226).

FLORENTINE T-BONE STEAK
Bistecca alla fiorentina

There is no dish that typifies Florentine cooking more famously than bistecca alla fiorentina. *Any trip to the city will provide ample opportunity to try it — it is on the menu in virtually every restaurant and* trattoria. *Sometimes referred to as porterhouse, the distinctive T-shaped bone separates two beautifully thick flanks of meat, which means that these steaks are always huge. The average weight of those we serve at BRUTTO is around 800g, but a Florentine friend told me that it's not considered truly Florentine unless it's over a kilo. One of our Tuscan waiters reckons his parents regularly share a 2-kilo steak between them.*

In Florence, the tradition is to cook these massive chops very rare, almost blue, in fact. I'm not keen on blue steak — it tends to be very difficult to cut and chew — so we cook ours rare to medium-rare, still bloody but easier to manage and delicious. The trick is to make sure you only buy 30-day-aged meat and to obey two other rules: remove the steak from the fridge at least half an hour before you want to cook it, and rest for at least 15 minutes after grilling. Otherwise the meat feels tough and you end up with a puddle of blood.

The other advice I have been given is to consider heat as a seasoning. Apart from the steak, there are only two other elements here: fire and salt. This is best cooked on a barbecue, but you must get your charcoal extremely hot and make sure you haven't used any firelighters. These can impart a horrible chemical taint to the meat. Practise your barbecue lighting with natural methods like bound straw bundles or even twisted newspaper. If you don't have the luxury of a great barbecue, you could pan-fry, but expect a huge amount of heat and smoke, so you need to open all doors and windows and you'd probably be better off removing the battery from your smoke detector. Just don't forget to replace it afterwards ...

For one steak, enough for two to share:
800g–1kg T-bone (porterhouse) steak
flaky sea salt

Remove the steak from the fridge 30 minutes before you want to cook it. Fire up the barbecue. When it's so hot that you can't hold your hand 25cm above it without feeling uncomfortable, place the steak on the grill. Leave for 5 or 6 minutes. Turn it over and do the same on the other side. Then stand it upright and allow it to cook vertically for 3 or 4 minutes. If you are pan-frying, follow the same instructions using a large non-stick frying pan. Don't be tempted to use oil at any stage. The meat will not stick.

Press the meat with your finger. It should feel like muscle, not like soft flesh.

Transfer it to a chopping board and leave for 15 minutes, loosely covered with foil. Then remove the foil and cut the meat into large bite-sized pieces from the bone. Transfer to a warmed sharing plate, placing the meat either side of the bone to recreate the shape of the steak, and cover both sides with liberal amounts of crushed flaky sea salt. Traditionally *bistecca* are seasoned afterwards, not before. Serve with a simple green salad like the one on page 120, and leave olive oil on the table for those that want to add a little to the steak. These steaks are never served with sauce.

SLICED RARE BEEF LOIN
'Rosbif'

When we collect our massive bistecca *loins from our butcher in Smithfield Market and cut the T-bone steaks with a huge saw, and trim to prepare for our daily board of steak specials, we are left with around a kilo of fillet. This is effectively topside, a lovely cut of meat that we roast slowly and slice rare to serve with roasted potatoes. It's not dissimilar to a classic Sunday roast. We serve with pan juices and it's a Florentine classic, first spotted at Trattoria Sabatino in San Frediano just beyond the old city walls (page 303).*

For four to six:
4 tablespoons lard
1kg topside
flaky sea salt
200ml red wine
50ml chicken stock (page 205)
roasted potatoes from page 197

Preheat the oven to 150°C.

Put your largest frying pan on a high heat and melt the lard. Sear the topside on all sides in the pan until brown, then rest for 10 minutes. After the rest, transfer to a roasting tin. Sprinkle with salt and put into the oven for 12 minutes, then turn down to 110°C for 10 minutes. Use a meat thermometer to check the temperature – it should be a reliable 42°C at core. Remove to a chopping board and rest for 30 minutes, loosely covered with foil.

Meanwhile, transfer the cooking juices from the roasting tin to a large frying pan and add the red wine and chicken stock. Bubble fiercely until reduced by half.

Slice the beef and lay on warmed plates with the reduced cooking liquor and the roasted potatoes.

ROASTED COURGETTES WITH BORLOTTI BEANS & GREEN SAUCE

Zucchini arrostiti con borlotti e salsa verde

In spring, when courgettes are abundant and easy to get in all their varieties, my children complain. 'When will it stop?' they ask. Every morning I go to my veg patch and cut off the new day's little fingers and incorporate them into that day's meal.

Likewise borlotti beans. They're usually ready to pick when their pods turn papery and thin, otherwise the beans are too pale and don't have that wonderful mottled red and cream pattern. If you don't grow, please pick up the fresh borlotti beans at your favourite grocer or farmers' market.

For four:
1kg borlotti beans (to yield 500g when podded)
800g assorted courgettes, all shapes and colours
extra virgin olive oil
flaky sea salt
1 clove of garlic, very finely chopped
a handful of flat parsley leaves, finely chopped
80ml *salsa verde* (page 210), at room temperature
black pepper

Pod the borlotti beans, put them into a large saucepan of water and bring to the boil. Cook for 30 minutes. Leave them in the hot water off the boil while you prepare the other ingredients.

Top and tail the courgettes, chop roughly into interesting chunky shapes and sauté gently in several glugs of oil in your widest frying pan with a few pinches of salt, the chopped garlic and half the chopped parsley for about 10 minutes until almost tender.

Drain the warm borlotti beans and distribute between four warmed plates. Drizzle with olive oil. Place the cooked courgettes evenly on the borlotti. Slather the *salsa verde* and scatter the remaining chopped parsley, with a little drizzle of olive oil and a twist of black pepper.

LAMB CHOPS WRAPPED IN PAPER

Cotolette di agnello in cartoccio

This is a lovely spring dish when new-season lamb arrives in the butcher's shops. When lambs are around six months old, in September or October, the flesh has a fuller flavour, more meaty and less milky, so it's a great dish for autumn, too.

This preparation adds a little theatricality when the individual parcels are opened, releasing a fragrant puff of steam.

For four:
2 ripe, medium tomatoes, quartered
4 small onions, peeled and halved
flaky sea salt
extra virgin olive oil
8 lamb chops
16 tinned anchovy fillets
a handful of green beans, trimmed
2 cloves of garlic, very finely sliced
a small handful of oregano leaves
black pepper

Preheat the oven to 180°C.

Take four very large squares of greaseproof paper, and evenly distribute the tomatoes and onions between them, with a good pinch of salt. Heat a frying pan and add a good glug or two of olive oil. When the oil is hot, brown the lamb chops, no more than a minute each side.

Now lay 2 chops in the centre of each sheet, with 2 anchovy fillets on top of the meat, and evenly share out the green beans. Scatter over the sliced garlic and oregano leaves. Season with sea salt and pepper and drizzle well with olive oil. Carefully gather the sides of the greaseproof paper and fold tightly to create closed parcels.

Place the parcels on a large baking sheet and cook in the oven for 15 minutes. Serve immediately on flat plates and let everyone work out what to do.

CHICKEN WITH GRAPES, OLIVES & SAGE

Pollo con uva, olive e salvia

There is something quite satisfying about combining the two main fruit crops of the region — grapes and olives — and using them in the same dish. There's a winning contrast between the sweetness of one and the brackish tang of the other. I think it looks more impressive to leave the grapes attached to the fine stems of the small bunches, but only if they are not too twiggy. If they are, pick the grapes off and discard the stems.

Ask your butcher to cut the whole bird into eight roughly even pieces.

For four:
extra virgin olive oil
1 small onion, finely sliced
1 small carrot, peeled and finely sliced
1 celery stalk, finely sliced
1 large free-range chicken, around 1.5kg, cut into 8 pieces
flaky sea salt
black pepper
a large bunch of small, sweet, seedless grapes
a large handful of Taggiasca olives, pitted
2 cloves of garlic, peeled and cut in half lengthways
a large handful of sage leaves
200ml white wine

Preheat the oven to 180°C.

Heat several good glugs of olive oil in a very large, cast-iron, ovenproof casserole dish. Soften the onion, carrot and celery for about 10 minutes. Season the chicken pieces with salt and pepper and add to the pan. Cook for another 12–15 minutes until the chicken is nicely golden brown. Reduce the heat and add the grapes, olives, garlic and sage leaves. Stir for a few minutes. Pour in two-thirds of the white wine and place the casserole dish uncovered in the oven for 30 minutes.

At the 30-minute point, check the contents and if still too wet, turn the oven up to 200°C for a further 10 minutes. Transfer the chicken, olives and grapes to a large serving dish with the garlic and sticky sage leaves and cover. Place the casserole dish on a high heat and deglaze the cooking juices with the rest of the white wine for a few minutes until reduced to a sticky sauce. Pour it over the chicken and serve.

FRIED CHICKEN
Pollo fritto alla fiorentina

*There is a fair amount of frying in Florentine kitchens, with the most famous fried dish being
fritto misto di carne — mixed fried meats. I wanted to include this popular version using chicken
rather than the heavy, meaty traditional iteration. This was firstly to add something lighter
(in as much as fried chicken can be called 'light'), but also because it's a great dish to enjoy on
summer days with lots of fresh lemons and a scattering of fragrant rosemary. You could make
the marinade and leave the covered raw chicken in the fridge overnight for more flavour, or start
your preparations in the morning, as long as the chicken has at least 2 hours to marinate.*

For four:
4 free-range chicken breasts, skinless
4 small free-range chicken legs, skinless
3 lemons
2 sprigs of rosemary
1 clove of garlic, quartered
100ml extra virgin olive oil, perhaps more
150g '00' flour
2 large free-range eggs, whisked
1 litre vegetable oil, for frying
flaky sea salt

Cut the breasts into thirds and separate the drumsticks from the thighs. Cut the thighs
in half. Place all the chicken pieces in a large bowl with one of the lemons, quartered
and squeezed, one sprig of rosemary and the quartered garlic clove. Cover with the
olive oil and leave in the fridge overnight or for at least 2 hours. Take out of the fridge
30 minutes before you want to start frying, remove the chicken pieces and shake off the
excess oil.

Put the flour on a large plate and the whisked eggs into a wide bowl. Dip the chicken
into the beaten egg, letting any excess egg drip off, then roll in the flour, shaking off the
excess. Set aside.

Heat the vegetable oil to 170°C, so that when you drop a small cube of bread into it the
bread turns light brown in about 15 seconds. If it goes too dark, the oil is too hot and
you'll need to adjust accordingly.

Fry the chicken pieces, in batches if necessary, for 12–15 minutes until golden brown.
Transfer to kitchen paper to drain. Place on a large, warmed platter, and scatter the
rosemary leaves picked from the remaining sprig and a few crunches of flaky sea salt.
Serve immediately with the other 2 lemons, quartered.

FRIED RED MULLET & ASPARAGUS WITH PARSLEY, GARLIC & LEMON ZEST
Triglia e asparagi fritti con gremolata

The western coastal city of Livorno is the closest the sea gets to Florence, at a distance of around 90 kilometres. It's known for its excellent seafood, and much of the fish you will find in the small handful of fishmonger stalls in Florence's Central Market will have made the hour and a half journey from the early morning catch to the residential lunch and dinner tables of the city, still as fresh as if you were eating it harbour-side. It's quite difficult to find fish on the menus of restaurants and trattorie, *but the locals enjoy a change from time to time.*

For four:
16 slender asparagus spears
8 small red mullet, gutted and cleaned but whole
75g '00' flour
75g semolina
whole milk
flaky sea salt
1 litre vegetable oil, for frying
1 lemon

For the gremolata:
a handful of flat parsley leaves, chopped finely
1 small clove of garlic, very finely chopped
zest of 1 lemon
extra virgin olive oil

Mix the parsley, garlic and lemon zest together. Gremolata is normally just this – a dry accompaniment – but I'm asking you to cheat by adding a teaspoonful or two of olive oil. I just hope the food police don't find out. Mix well and set aside.

Trim the woody stems from the asparagus spears and discard. Slice any particularly thick stems lengthways. Then cut them into pieces the same length as the fish.

Combine the two flours and place on a large plate. Fill a wide bowl with milk. Crunch some salt flakes on to each of the red mullet. Dip each in the milk and shake off any excess. Now dredge them in the flour mix. Do the same for the asparagus.

Heat the oil to 170°C, checking it's ready by dropping a small cube of bread into it. It should turn light brown in 15 seconds. Deep-fry the asparagus for 2–3 minutes, then remove with tongs. Lay on kitchen paper. Deep-fry the red mullet for about 4 minutes, until golden brown. Carefully remove with a fish slice and lay on kitchen paper. Arrange the fish and asparagus spears on a pretty serving platter and liberally scatter over the illegal gremolata. Serve with the lemon, cut into wedges.

ROASTED SEASONAL VEGETABLES WITH COUNTRY HERBS

Verdure di stagione arrosto

Sometimes it's good to let the vegetables do the hard work. They've been growing for months, some of them through the winter, and maturing at different rates to come together just when you need them. The ingredients in this simple country dish will all be available in spring and summer but they are also supermarket staples throughout the year. You can play around with the composition, but adding and subtracting will require you to think about cooking times. All the vegetables should still have some bite — you really don't want anything to be mushy and overcooked.

For four:
12 small, waxy potatoes, washed but not peeled
2 fennel bulbs
12 asparagus spears, woody stalks removed
1 aubergine, topped and tailed
flaky sea salt
extra virgin olive oil
2 red onions, thickly sliced
2 cloves of garlic, peeled and each cut in half
12 baby carrots, washed but not peeled
4 sprigs of thyme
2 sprigs of rosemary
black pepper
a small handful of oregano leaves
a small handful of sage leaves

Place a pan of salted water on the hob and bring to the boil. Halve any large potatoes, then add them all to the pan and cook for 10 minutes. Remove, drain and rinse in cold water. Set aside.

Preheat the oven to 180°C.

Slice each fennel bulb into sixths, lengthways. Cut each asparagus spear in half, horizontally. Slice the aubergine into 2cm discs and salt immediately.

Place a large roasting tray in the oven with several glugs of olive oil. When it's hot, after about 3 minutes, add the fennel, onion, garlic, potatoes and carrots to the tray, with the thyme and rosemary sprigs, generous pinches of salt and twists of pepper and return to the oven for 10 minutes. Remove, shake thoroughly, and add the asparagus, aubergine, oregano and sage. Add more oil if it's looking dry or the vegetables are sticking to the pan, and loosen with a wooden spatula if necessary. Continue to roast for another 10–12 minutes.

Take the tray from the oven, transfer to a serving dish if you prefer, but personally I like putting the blackened and rustic roasting tray right down in the centre of the table with cooking tongs and all the burnt herbs on show. Sprinkle with a little more sea salt and a drizzle of olive oil just before serving.

RIBBONS OF BEEF WITH WILTED BITTER LEAVES

Tagliata di manzo con radicchio

The variations of steak preparation in Florence and beyond prove how important beef is to the region. Tagliata – strips or ribbons – makes a dish that is less daunting than a huge slab of meat and easier to eat with just a fork. The result is more salad-like and somehow lighter but without compromising on succulence and flavour. This is best made with very good-quality sirloins, already cut into flat steak shapes. Look for the higher-welfare, 30-day-aged beef and make sure you remove it from the fridge half an hour before you want to cook.

For four:
1 head of radicchio – Treviso or Chioggia
extra virgin olive oil
2 × 400g sirloin steaks
flaky sea salt
black pepper
a handful of flat parsley leaves, finely chopped

Remove the hard base of the radicchio and slice the leaves into ribbons. Set aside.

Heat a few glugs of olive oil in a very large frying pan over a high heat, season each side of the steaks with salt and pepper, and sear on all sides, including the strip of fat, until nicely browned. About 2 minutes. Turn the heat down a little and cook for a further 4–5 minutes, turning frequently. If you like, you can make a little incision to check the colour of the meat inside. It should be very pink but not blue. Remove from the pan and rest for 5 minutes.

Meanwhile, add a splash more oil to the same pan and gently cook the shredded radicchio in the meat juices. Wilt for around 4 minutes, stirring and tossing. Remove from the heat and drain any excess oil.

Remove and discard the fat from the steaks, then slice into fine ribbons. Place the wilted radicchio on four warmed plates and evenly distribute the slices of pink, juicy steak. Add a twist of black pepper and a scattering of chopped parsley.

FLORENTINE SALT COD WITH TOMATOES

Baccalà alla livornese

Let me start by apologising for the contradiction in the title of this recipe. How can something be Florentine if it's from Livorno? Well, this is as close as you'll get these days to a typical fish dish in Florence, I'm afraid. In centuries gone by, the River Arno provided plentiful freshwater fish for the city's markets, kitchens and dining tables, but pollution from the leather tanning industry probably put paid to that. Salt cod is widely available outside Italy in Italian and Spanish delis, and I have even seen it hanging up in Caribbean fishmongers near my house in south-east London. I prefer it to fresh cod, which is terribly over-fished currently, but it needs to be washed and rinsed thoroughly to remove the large amounts of preserving salt. You should begin preparing this dish the day before.

For four:
700–800g dried salt cod
extra virgin olive oil
1 large white onion, finely sliced
1 clove of garlic, finely sliced
1 × 400g tin of chopped Italian tomatoes
100g '00' flour, salted
a handful of flat parsley leaves, finely chopped
black pepper

The day before you want to cook, cover the dried salt cod with plenty of cold water and soak for at least 24 hours. Change the water three or four times during this period. Finally, rinse once more and pat dry.

Place a large saucepan over a medium heat and add a few glugs of olive oil. Gently sauté the sliced onion for about 10 minutes until soft and translucent, being careful not to colour. Add the sliced garlic and cook for another 2 minutes. Now add the tinned chopped tomatoes and stir thoroughly, reducing the heat to a simmer. Cook and stir for 15 minutes or so until it resembles a smooth sauce.

Cut the rinsed cod into bite-sized pieces and heat another glug or two of olive oil in a large frying pan. Dredge the cod in the flour, shake off any excess, and fry for a minute or two on each side until golden brown. Remove and drain on kitchen paper.

Transfer the fried cod pieces to the tomato sauce, cook gently for 4–5 minutes, then remove from the heat. Allow to rest for a further 5 minutes (this dish is often served at room temperature), then distribute between four plates, with a scattering of chopped parsley and a twist of black pepper.

FRIED SQUID & COURGETTE
Frittura di calamari e zucchine

Squid is a popular market ingredient in Florence. It's also readily available in fishmongers everywhere. It's so easy to cook, but I think some people are put off by the fiddly cleaning and preparation. If you're daunted by the prospect (you shouldn't be), then your fishmonger will happily clean them and remove the gladius. The batter I use in this recipe is particularly light and has more in common with tempura.

For four:
4 medium squid, cleaned
4 medium courgettes
4 free-range egg whites
250ml sparkling water
200g '00' flour
fine salt
1 litre vegetable oil, for frying
flaky sea salt
1 lemon

Rinse the cleaned squid in cold running water to remove any sticky surface build-up. Pull the tentacles from inside the body. Remove and discard the hard, plasticky gladius and the ink sac if there is one. Cut off and discard the tough bit below the tentacles. Cut off and keep the wings, slice them in half, slice the body into rings, then place the remaining tentacles, wings and rings on kitchen paper to drain.

Top and tail the courgettes and cut lengthways into thick matchsticks around 5cm long.

Whisk the egg whites and sparkling water together in a large bowl and put the flour mixed with a good pinch of fine salt on a large plate.

Heat the oil in a large saucepan to 180°C, or until a small cube of bread turns brown in 20–30 seconds.

Dip the squid pieces and courgettes, one handful at a time, into the egg and fizzy water mix and then dredge in the flour. Shake off any excess and fry in batches for a minute or two until golden brown. Transfer to kitchen paper with a slotted spoon.

Serve on a large platter for sharing, with a final crunch of sea salt flakes and the lemon cut into quarters.

FLORENTINE MEATLOAF
Polpettone alla fiorentina

Polpettone are very large meatballs and a staple of regional home cooking all over Italy. I've seen them stuffed with mozzarella, sometimes with spinach and even with whole hard-boiled eggs. But the Florentine version is made much more simply, usually with veal and not filled. It is shaped into an elongated sphere, a little like a very fat sausage, and sliced at the table. In other parts of Tuscany it is made with a tomato sauce, but I like it with the cooking juices and the braised soffritto from the pan. It goes very well with mashed potato.

For four:
80g crustless stale bread, broken into small pieces
500g minced veal
80g mortadella, chopped very finely
50g grated Parmesan
1 large free-range egg
½ teaspoon freshly grated nutmeg
a small handful of flat parsley leaves, chopped
flaky sea salt
black pepper
'00' flour, for dusting
extra virgin olive oil
1 onion, sliced
1 carrot, peeled and diced
1 celery stalk, finely sliced
1 bay leaf
150ml white wine
200ml chicken stock (page 205), or ½ a stock cube dissolved in 200ml boiled water
juice of ½ a lemon

Start by soaking the bread in warm water for 20 minutes, then squeeze out all the moisture and place in a bowl with the minced veal, the chopped mortadella, the grated Parmesan and the egg. Using your hands, squash all the ingredients together, adding the freshly grated nutmeg, chopped parsley, a good pinch of salt and a twist of black pepper. Transfer to a clean work surface and wet your hands with cold water. Form the mixture into a thick, rounded oval shape. Very lightly dust with flour. Heat a few glugs of olive oil in a very large frying pan and carefully add the meatloaf, turning slowly to make sure all sides are nicely browned, then gently remove and set aside.

Place a large, cast-iron casserole dish for which you have a lid on a medium heat and gently sauté the onion, carrot and celery in a few glugs of olive oil for 10 minutes until glossy and soft. Carefully introduce the meatloaf to the casserole dish with the bay leaf and the wine. Cover and cook for 1–1¼ hours, adding stock a little at a time during the process, never letting it dry out but never flooding it either.

Remove the meatloaf to a warmed serving platter and turn up the heat under the casserole dish. Add the lemon juice, reduce until a little more syrupy, then remove the bay leaf and take off the heat.

Slice the meatloaf, pour over the *soffritto* and pan juices and serve, perhaps with a generous dollop of buttery mashed potatoes.

VEAL & PEA STEW
Stufato di vitello con piselli

Veal is the milky meat from calves born in late spring, so it makes seasonal sense to combine it with fresh, late spring vegetables like peas. The yield from peas in their pods, particularly early peas harvested in April in Italy (May to June in more northern climates), which tend to be smaller, is a little disheartening. A whole kilo of un-podded young peas sometimes only returns 300g, and when you factor in the collateral damage caused by the thieving podder (I have never known anyone podding peas not to help themselves to a few handfuls) it might be less. If you can find a small child to help with the podding, even better.

For four:
extra virgin olive oil
1 onion, finely sliced
1 carrot, peeled and finely sliced
1 celery stalk, finely sliced
1 clove of garlic, chopped
flaky sea salt
800g stewing veal, chopped into bite-sized pieces
'00' flour, for coating
150ml red wine
4 tablespoons tomato purée
a handful of basil leaves
350ml *brodo* (page 202), or water
1.5kg peas in their pods (to yield 600g when podded)
1 small child (optional)
black pepper

Heat a few good glugs of olive oil in a very large cast-iron saucepan with a lid (Le Creuset pans are perfect, aren't they?) and gently sauté the onion, carrot, celery and garlic for 10–12 minutes until soft and glossy. Add a pinch of salt. Don't let anything burn.

Dust the veal chunks lightly with flour and put them into the pan until browned, turning from time to time. Pour in the wine, stir and cover, reducing the heat if necessary, until the wine has mostly been evaporated. About 12–15 minutes.

Add the tomato purée and half the basil, stir to combine everything, then pour in the *brodo* (or water), cover again, and cook on a low heat for about 2 hours, topping up with boiled water to keep the consistency stew-like but never soupy. At the 2-hour mark, add the peas and the remaining basil, test the seasoning and adjust if necessary. Cook for 10 minutes more, then remove from the heat and let it rest for a further 10 minutes.

Serve in warmed bowls, with a twist of black pepper and some crusty bread. Or even better, garlic bread.

FRIED BREADED VEAL FILLETS
Vitello milanese

Not a local dish, obviously (the clue is in the name), but it is very popular in the restaurants of Florence nonetheless. It's one of those comfort classics that transcend the focus on regionality, and it has become an adopted recipe pretty much everywhere in Italy. One of my favourite trattorie, Cammillo in Oltrarno (page 302), does an excellent version that I have tried to replicate here.

For four:
4 veal escalopes
2 large free-range eggs
150g '00' flour, seasoned with fine salt
300g panko breadcrumbs
a large knob of butter
extra virgin olive oil
flaky sea salt
black pepper
green salad, for serving (page 120)
2 lemons, halved, for serving

Place the veal escalopes under clingfilm and gently flatten with a rolling pin until just under 1cm thick.

Lightly whisk the eggs and place in a wide bowl. Empty the flour on to a large plate and the breadcrumbs on to a separate large plate. Line them up in the following order: flour, eggs, breadcrumbs.

Heat half the butter and a good glug of olive oil in a very large frying pan. Dip the escalopes into the flour, shake off any excess, then into the egg, then the breadcrumbs, shaking off any excess again, and fry for 3 minutes on each side until golden and crisp. Add the remaining butter and more oil if needed for the others as you go. Drain on kitchen paper. Serve with a scattering of sea salt flakes and a twist of black pepper.

Serve on warmed plates, with green salad and the lemon halves.

BOILED BRISKET & TONGUE WITH GREEN SAUCE
Bollito misto con salsa verde

There are few more authentic Florentine dishes than bollito misto. *Last time I was at Nerbone in Florence's Mercato Centrale (page 296), the chef at this tiny tripe stall told me that although the tourists flock every day for the* lampredotto *roll, the locals come for bollito — by far the preferred meaty fix and a lot more refined and elegant, in my opinion.*
     Start this one day before you want to serve.

For four:
800g beef brisket
1 medium ox tongue, brined
4 carrots, peeled and sliced lengthways
1 large onion, peeled and studded with 6 cloves
2 celery stalks, halved
10 whole peppercorns
1 bay leaf
a small handful of parsley stalks
a small handful of thyme
a small handful of rosemary
flaky sea salt
black pepper (optional)
6 tablespoons *salsa verde* (page 210)

Put the brisket, tongue, carrots, onion and celery into a very large saucepan. Make a little muslin parcel for the peppercorns, bay leaf, parsley stalks, thyme and rosemary, then tie the parcel tightly with string and pop it into the saucepan. Cover with a generous amount of cold water. Bring to the boil briefly, then turn down the heat and simmer for about 2 hours.

Remove the brisket and tongue and allow to cool. Remove and discard the carrot, onion and celery. While the tongue is still warm, peel off and discard the skin. Strain the cooking stock through muslin placed in a large sieve into a jug and discard the herb parcel. When cooled, place the tongue and brisket (covered with foil) and the jug of stock in the fridge.

Next day, remove everything from the fridge. Peel the tongue if it still has a secondary skin and slice it into 1cm pieces. Slice the brisket similarly. Remove any scum from the stock, then carefully pass it through a sieve lined with muslin. Heat the liquid in a very large saucepan. Add the sliced meats with a good pinch or two of salt. Simmer for 12–15 minutes. Test the seasoning and adjust if necessary.

Evenly distribute the meats between four wide, warmed bowls and pour over the clear broth. Add a good smattering of *salsa verde* on top and serve while piping hot.

CONT

Side dishes are somewhat anomalous in Italy. The four-course structure of the classic *trattoria* menu means that your meal is already complete without the addition of extra vegetables or potatoes, particularly if you start with small bar snacks, too. But at BRUTTO we have found that they are very popular as an accompaniment to those *secondi* dishes if you decide to skip the pasta course. They are also a great addition to a feast-style meal, arranged on the banquet table to share, allowing everyone to have a small taste of a variety of flavours.

As always with Tuscan cooking, simplicity is the order of the day and seasonality dictates what ingredients you use to embellish your meal. Quite often, side dishes will consist of sliced, ripe tomatoes with plenty of salt and good olive oil, or a lightly dressed green salad. Vegetables like courgettes, always in great abundance during spring and summer, can be cut and lightly fried with mint leaves and salt. But there are other traditions from the Florentine canon that are worth making an effort for, such as the wonderful peas with pancetta or the cheesy, eggy, baked spinach.

I'm not a fan of the neat little plates you tend to see used in restaurants to serve side dishes. It's much more impressive and generous to use large serving platters and huge bowls placed at the centre of the table to convey the sense of an abundant feast.

ORNI

FLORENTINE PEAS WITH PANCETTA
Piselli alla fiorentina

This wonderful contorno *is something you can make all year round if you substitute fresh peas with frozen ones. It's sometimes frowned upon in cheffy circles to use frozen peas but I've done so many times and the results are excellent.*

As with many Tuscan dishes, it is often served at room temperature, particularly on a hot day.

For four:
extra virgin olive oil
250g unsmoked pancetta, cut into short matchsticks or small cubes
1 clove of garlic, very finely sliced
1.5–2kg peas in their pods (to yield 600–800g when podded)
flaky sea salt
black pepper
150ml chicken stock (page 205)
a good handful of flat parsley leaves, roughly chopped

Pour a little olive oil, just enough to barely coat, into a large, heavy-based saucepan over a low to medium heat. (Don't be tempted to use more olive oil than this otherwise the pancetta will poach. It releases plenty of its own fat while cooking.) Add the pancetta and the garlic. Heat and stir for 3 minutes but make sure the garlic does not brown. Lower the heat if necessary.

Add the peas with a good pinch or two of sea salt and a generous twist of black pepper. Stir to make sure the peas are coated with the pancetta fat and olive oil. Add the stock, adjust the heat to a gentle simmer, stir, cover, and cook for 15 minutes. Remove the lid, stir and check the seasoning. Add the chopped parsley and stir. If there is still a pool of stock, cook it off for a further 4–5 minutes.

Serve in a very large, pretty dish with a further drizzle of olive oil.

GREEN BEANS WITH EXCELLENT OLIVE OIL
Fagioli verdi

We are accustomed to green beans, particularly in the UK, cooked until they are soft and served steaming hot with lashings of butter. That nursery preparation rather kills the vibrant flavours this subtle vegetable has to offer. Whether they are French beans, dwarf beans, fine beans, bobby beans, string beans or any other of the green variety, they all have the same wonderful grassy taste of chlorophyll and antioxidants which should be savoured. Green beans should never be mushy once cooked, but nor should they be too firm and squeaky on the teeth. By serving this dish at room temperature, I find the flavour comes through even more than when hot. Use your best olive oil, please.

For four:
ice cubes
800g green beans, trimmed
flaky sea salt
black pepper
excellent extra virgin olive oil

Prepare a large bowl of cold water with a full tray of ice cubes popped in.

Place a pan of very well-salted water on a high heat and bring to the boil. Add the trimmed green beans and boil at full throttle for no more than 4 minutes if they are thin or 5 minutes if they are fatter.

Drain the beans in a sieve, rinse under a cold running tap, then transfer to the iced water. Leave for 5 minutes, then drain again and transfer to a large serving bowl. Season with a good few pinches of salt and a twist or two of black pepper, drizzle generously with olive oil, toss carefully and serve.

RAW WHITE CABBAGE SLAW
Cavolo crudo

This was a thrilling surprise when I first had it a few summers ago in a small trattoria
*in San Frediano. I was instructed by a friend not to mention the place by name because it's
a cherished neighbourhood secret and the locals would kill me. (It's Sabatino, by the way –
page 303. Apologies to my friend and the locals.) When you have a single-ingredient dish
which also happens to be raw, there's nowhere to hide, so you'd better make sure your produce
is excellent and your preparation is careful and sympathetic. It has to be made to order just
before you want to serve it.*

For four:
1 whole white cabbage
flaky sea salt
black pepper
juice of ½ a lemon
extra virgin olive oil

Remove the outer leaves of the cabbage and discard. Using an extremely sharp knife,
slice the cabbage as thinly as possible. You could also use a mandoline. Pick up the
finely shredded strands of cabbage and pile them high on a very large serving platter.
Dress with several crunches of sea salt, a few twists of black pepper, the lemon juice
evenly sprinkled and a long drizzle of olive oil. Don't worry about the layers of raw
cabbage underneath, gravity and movement will make sure the whole pile gets treated,
albeit slightly differently. It's part of the pleasure of this dish. Large salad tossers
are essential.

WHITE BEANS WITH OLIVE OIL
Cannellini

I'd like to take a gamble, I'm even prepared to bet real money, that this dish is on every trattoria *menu in Florence. It's wonderful simplicity at its best. You should always use organic dried beans and soak them overnight in plenty of cold water. Do not be tempted to add salt to the soaking water — it will make the beans hard and unpleasant.*

For four:
400g dried cannellini beans
1 onion, peeled
1 large carrot, peeled
1 celery stalk
1 bay leaf
flaky sea salt
extra virgin olive oil
black pepper (optional)

Start the day before. Put the dried beans into a very large vessel and completely cover with cold water. Do not add salt.

Next day, drain and rinse under a cold tap for a minute or two.

Place a very large pan of water on a high heat and bring to the boil. Cut the onion in half horizontally so the root and top are intact. Cut the carrot in half lengthways. Cut the celery in half. Add all these to the boiling water with the drained beans and the bay leaf. Do not add salt. Once boiling again, reduce to a simmer and allow to bubble gently for 2–3 hours until soft and creamy, topping up the water when necessary. *Only now*, once cooked, can you add a few pinches of salt and let the beans cool in the stock. Remove the onion, carrot, celery and bay leaf and discard.

Drain the beans, place in a large serving bowl with a good drizzle of olive oil and a crunch more sea salt. Add a twist of black pepper if you like, but I prefer them without.

WHITE BEANS IN TOMATO SAUCE
Fagioli all'uccelletto

The curious Italian name for this dish, which I have only ever seen in Florence, translates as 'beans of the little birds'. This is a nod to the fact that game birds are traditionally served with the same sauce of tomato, garlic and sage. It's the perfect accompaniment to any grilled or roasted meat or fowl, but also delicious in this authentic Florentine version of 'baked beans'.

For four:
400g dried cannellini beans
1 onion, peeled
1 large carrot, peeled
1 celery stalk
1 bay leaf
flaky sea salt
2 cloves of garlic, peeled
extra virgin olive oil
a handful of sage leaves
300g passata
black pepper

Start the day before. Put the dried beans into a very large vessel and completely cover with cold water. Do not add salt.

Next day, drain and rinse under a cold tap for a minute or two.

Place a very large pan of water on a high heat and bring to the boil. Cut the onion in half horizontally so the root and top are intact. Cut the carrot in half lengthways. Cut the celery in half. Add all these to the boiling water with the drained beans and the bay leaf. Do not add salt. Once boiling again, reduce to a simmer and allow to bubble gently for 2–3 hours until soft and creamy, topping up the water when necessary. *Only now*, once cooked, can you add a few pinches of salt and leave the beans in the stock while you make the tomato sauce, remembering to remove and discard the onion, carrot, celery and bay leaf.

Slice the garlic extremely finely and gently sauté in a few glugs of olive oil in a very large saucepan. Do not let it brown. Shred the sage leaves with a sharp knife, add to the pan, and pour in the passata. Season with a pinch of salt and a twist of pepper and bring to a bubble. Simmer for 5 minutes while stirring. Now add the drained cannellini beans, stir, and simmer for a few moments more, testing and adjusting the seasoning if necessary.

Place in a large bowl with a serving spoon and add to your table feast of roasts and grills.

SPINACH COOKED IN THE OVEN
Sformato alla fiorentina

Here's that Catherine de' Medici influence again. The Florentine queen really did like her spinach. Sformato, a lovely word, means flan, and I've had this before, cooked for longer, as a sort of spinach quiche. But in this version the dish comes out of the oven moist and creamy – much easier to spoon on to your plate to accompany a simple piece of grilled meat or fish.

For four:
1kg baby spinach, washed thoroughly
2 medium free-range eggs
350ml double cream
100g grated Parmesan
flaky sea salt
black pepper
nutmeg

Preheat the oven to 180°C.

Cook the spinach in plenty of salted boiling water until it has collapsed, about 90 seconds maximum. Drain and squeeze all the water out. Place on a chopping board and chop roughly. Set aside.

Mix the eggs, cream and Parmesan together with a fork in a large mixing bowl. Add a pinch of salt, a twist of black pepper and a couple of gratings from the nutmeg. Stir in the chopped spinach. Transfer the mixture to an ovenproof dish and place on the middle shelf of the preheated oven for 20–25 minutes until the top is just starting to turn brown. Serve with a large metal spoon to make it easier to break through the slight crust to the moist, cheesy spinach below.

LENTILS
Lenticche

Lentils are a great accompaniment to simple rustic meat dishes like bollito misto *(page 173).*
They are always served at New Year with delicious, sticky cotechino sausage to bring good
luck and fortune − the small discs are said to represent coins.

    When dicing the onion, carrot and celery, make the pieces as small as you can so they
are the same size as the tiny green lentils. It's a good opportunity to practise your knife skills.

    (At BRUTTO we serve these lentils with plump pork and fennel sausages bought
from our local Italian deli. Quick recipe: Roast or fry the sausages until done, place them
on a generous pile of freshly cooked lentils, and finish off with an extremely large dollop
of Dijon mustard.)

For four:
300g green lentils
1 bay leaf
extra virgin olive oil
1 onion, extremely finely diced
1 carrot, peeled and extremely finely diced
1 celery stalk, extremely finely diced
1 clove of garlic, very finely chopped
flaky sea salt
a small handful of flat parsley, chopped
red wine vinegar
black pepper

Thoroughly rinse the lentils and drain in a sieve. Bring about 1.5 litres of *unsalted* cold
water to the boil and cook the lentils, with the bay leaf, for about 20–25 minutes until
soft but with a little firm bite when placed between your front teeth. Remove any scum
that comes to the surface. Drain and remove the bay leaf.

While the lentils are cooking, heat a good few glugs of olive oil in a very large saucepan
and gently sauté the onion, carrot, celery and garlic for 10–12 minutes with a pinch
of salt until soft and glossy. Add a glug more oil if it dries out. Now stir in the drained
lentils, the chopped parsley and mix thoroughly with a splash of red wine vinegar.
Stir for a few minutes more, take off the heat and serve with a twist of black pepper.

ASPARAGUS, RAW & COOKED, WITH PECORINO
Asparagi al vapore e crudi con Pecorino

This is a delightful way to serve asparagus, allowing the larger spears to develop in flavour in the steamer and the ribbons of raw asparagus to add freshness and texture. It's important to remove the woody stems until you see the green core of the spear at the base. Additionally, make a note of the width of your steamer so that you can cut the stems to the right size before cooking. When grating the Pecorino, use the sharp, rough edge of the box grater (the one you probably don't use very often). It creates really lovely crumbs of cheese rather than the delicate flakes of the other side.

For four:
24 asparagus spears
flaky sea salt
juice of ½ a lemon
extra virgin olive oil
black pepper
80g Pecorino, roughly grated

Place a large saucepan half-filled with water on the hob and bring to the boil. Make sure you have a well-fitting steamer to go on top.

Take 16 of the asparagus spears and, after removing the woody bases, trim the bottoms with a potato peeler to create an elegant taper that reveals the bright green core under the dark green skin. Make sure they are the right length to fit into the steamer and steam, covered, for 4–5 minutes.

Meanwhile, using the potato peeler, strip the remaining spears lengthways to create long ribbons thin enough to curl. Remove the steamed asparagus spears and place 4 on each plate. Evenly distribute the raw asparagus ribbons. Dress with crunches of flaky sea salt, lemon juice, a light drizzle of olive oil and a twist of pepper. Finally scatter over the roughly grated Pecorino and serve straight away.

FRIED TUSCAN MUSHROOMS
Porcini fritti

Tuscany is the home of the porcini mushroom and they appear on market stalls in the autumn (see photo opposite). They are gloriously dense and have a deep, funky flavour that few other varieties can match. The best way to enjoy them as a contorno *is to slice them lengthways, quite thickly, around 2cm, and shallow-fry them in olive oil with salt and chopped parsley and perhaps some finely chopped garlic. If you can find them, you can ignore this recipe. Same with chanterelles (aka girolles), shiitake and morels.*

You can still enjoy those widely available closed cup and chestnut varieties with this variation. It's a good way to impart a bit more flavour and texture.

For four:
16–20 closed cup or chestnut mushrooms
2 large free-range eggs
flaky sea salt
150g panko breadcrumbs
500ml olive oil
a small handful of flat parsley leaves, finely chopped

Slice the mushrooms in half lengthways or in four lengthways if they're particularly large, about 2cm thick.

Whisk the eggs and place in a shallow bowl with a pinch of salt. Put the breadcrumbs in a separate wide bowl.

Heat the oil in a very large frying pan. Dip the mushrooms into the whisked egg, shake off any excess, then lightly coat with the breadcrumbs. Fry in the oil for 1 or 2 minutes, turning over once or twice until they are golden and crisp. You may need to do this in batches. Lay them on kitchen paper while you're making the next batch.

Transfer to a large serving plate, scatter over the finely chopped parsley and serve while hot.

SMALL ROASTED POTATOES
Patate arrosto

*These are the perfect accompaniment to any meat, fowl or fish dish. They may remind you
of the traditional roast spuds you'll find on Sunday lunch tables all over the UK and in North
America, but in Florence they are always much smaller, thus providing more surface area to get
more of the best bit — the crunchy, salty crusts. Sometimes, when in season, new potatoes will
be used and this variation is just as lovely, with a smoother, nuttier and less floury texture inside.
(At BRUTTO we serve between 25kg and 30kg of roasted potatoes per day.)*

For four:
500g standard potatoes (Maris Piper, King Edward, etc.)
or
500g new potatoes, washed
extra virgin olive oil
sunflower oil
4 cloves of garlic, unpeeled
flaky sea salt
a large handful of rosemary leaves

Peel the potatoes and cut them into small triangular pieces. This is usually achieved
by cutting each potato in half and then cutting the halves into quarters. If using new
potatoes, don't peel them and simply cut them in half.

Preheat the oven to 190°C.

Place a large saucepan of salted water over a high heat and bring to the boil. Add the
potatoes and cook for 5–6 minutes, so they are still firm but can be pierced with the tip
of a sharp pointed knife. Drain in a colander.

Pour a few glugs of each oil into a large roasting tin and place in the oven for
3 or 4 minutes. Place the flat blade of a kitchen knife on each of the unpeeled garlic
cloves and hit firmly with the heel of your palm. Add the drained potatoes, the smashed
garlic cloves, a good pinch of salt and half the rosemary to the hot oil, shake the roasting
tin to coat the potatoes and return to the oven. After 30 minutes, remove and shake
again or turn the potatoes with tongs. After a further 30 minutes, do the same and add
the rest of the rosemary. If using new potatoes, use this opportunity to slightly squash
some of them with a wooden spatula. Continue to roast for another 10–15 minutes,
maybe a little more, maybe a little less, until the potatoes look golden and crisp.

Serve in a large bowl with a further few crunches of flaky salt.

BRO
PASTE &

A well-stocked pantry is key to running a successful domestic kitchen. As well as *all* the different types of rice and *all* the pasta shapes, there should be multiple bags of flour of *all* the varieties, sugars, dried fruit, dried pulses, nuts, grains, oils, tinned anchovies, at least six different vinegars … The list goes on and will never be complete, but it can be comprehensive enough to always have what you need to hand.

In addition, it's a great idea to freeze any unused stock if you want to potentially save time in the future when you suddenly realise you desperately need it. Having said that, I rather enjoy the process of making stock and anything that keeps me in the kitchen longer is fine by me.

Bear in mind that pasta dough and bread dough can both be kept in the fridge for a day or two wrapped in clingfilm – just remember to remove them 45 minutes or so before you want to use them.

And the incredibly useful classic sauces in this chapter have natural preservatives that keep them fresh and tasty for several days in clean jars with tight-fitting lids in the fridge.

I, SALSE, DISPENSA

MAMMA MIA

BEEF BONE BROTH
Brodo

This is the broth I mean whenever I refer to brodo. *It's so good you can drink it on its own in a cup or heat it in a small pan with* stelline *— that tiny star-shaped pasta — for a delicious soup. Ask your butcher to saw the bones in half if they're huge. You need them to fit into your stock pot.*

Makes about 2 litres:
500g beef bones
2 chicken wings
1 large onion, peeled
4 cloves
sunflower oil
1 large carrot, peeled and halved
1 celery stalk, halved

Preheat the oven to 180°C.

Put the bones and chicken wings into a roasting tin and place in the oven for 45 minutes, until nicely browned with some caramelisation at the ends where the bone marrow has oozed out. The wings may appear shrivelled but they'll be full of flavour.

Cut the onion in half horizontally, so that the root and head are still intact, and stud each half with 2 cloves.

Place a griddle pan on a high heat with a little oil and char the onion until slightly burnt.

Remove the roasted bones from the oven and transfer to a large stock pot with the onion, carrot and celery. Cover with boiling water from a kettle (about 1.5 litres) and place on a high heat. Add another 1.5 litres from a boiled kettle and bring to the boil for about 2 minutes. Reduce the heat, cover, and simmer for about 3 hours, or until reduced by one third.

Remove and discard the vegetables and the bones and drain the *brodo* through a large sieve lined with muslin into a second large pot. Allow the stock to cool and scrape the fat from the surface. Transfer to large plastic containers (old, clean ice-cream tubs are perfect) and store in the fridge for later use. Put into smaller lidded containers if you want to freeze it.

CHICKEN STOCK
Brodo di pollo

An easy stock but only if you have the carcass of a large chicken left over from a Sunday roast along with fresh chicken wings.

Makes about 2 litres:
1 large chicken carcass and fresh chicken wings, totalling 400–500g
1 bay leaf
6 parsley stalks
1 clove
6 peppercorns
a small palmful of thyme
1 large onion, peeled and halved
1 large carrot, peeled and halved
1 celery stalk, halved
1 heaped teaspoon fine salt

Preheat the oven to 180°C and roast the carcass and wings in a roasting tin for about 20 minutes.

Put the bay leaf, parsley stalks, clove, peppercorns and thyme into a large square of muslin and tie tightly with a piece of string to create a pouch.

Remove the roasted chicken carcass and wings from the oven and transfer to a large stock pot with the vegetables and the herb pouch. Add boiled water from a kettle and then a second, about 3 litres in total. Add the salt and bring to the boil. Reduce to a simmer and let the pot gently bubble for about 1–1½ hours, or until reduced by a third.

Remove and discard all the large pieces with tongs and strain the rest through a sieve into another large pot. Scrape any scum or fat off the surface and either use immediately or store in the fridge in large empty ice-cream tubs. You can freeze if you like in smaller batches.

VEGETABLE STOCK
Brodo di verdure

*The simplest stock of all to make and the subtlest in flavour. Perfect for vegetable soups,
light risottos and delicate sauces.*

Makes about 2 litres:
1 bay leaf
6 peppercorns
6 parsley stalks
a small palmful of thyme
2 large onions, peeled and halved
2 celery stalks, halved
2 large carrots, peeled and halved
1 fennel bulb, halved
1 large leek, washed, trimmed and quartered
1 heaped teaspoon fine salt

Place the bay leaf, peppercorns, parsley stalks and thyme in a large square of muslin,
create a pouch and tie firmly with a piece of string.

Put all the vegetables along with the herb pouch into a large stock pot and then pour
two boiled kettles of hot water, about 3 litres in total, into the pot. Place on a high
heat, add the salt, and bring to the boil. After 2 minutes, reduce to a simmer and allow
to simmer for about 1½ hours, or until reduced by one third.

Strain through a sieve into a second large pot, remove any scum from the surface and,
if not using immediately, store in plastic containers in the fridge or smaller batches
in the freezer.

GREEN SAUCE
Salsa verde

The is a simple but essential accompaniment for practically anything to which you want to add a piquant, salty, herby hit. We make it this way at BRUTTO, without anchovies and without breadcrumbs, so that it can be used for vegetarians and those with gluten intolerances.

Makes a quantity to fit into a clean, empty jam jar:
1 shallot
½ a clove of garlic
a large handful of flat parsley leaves
1 heaped teaspoon capers
1 teaspoon Dijon mustard
1 teaspoon lemon juice
1 tablespoon white wine vinegar
a pinch of fine salt
130ml extra virgin olive oil

Dice the shallot as finely as possible and chop the garlic as finely as possible. Chop the parsley several times in two or three directions and chop the capers roughly. Transfer from your chopping board into a medium bowl, add the mustard, lemon juice, vinegar, salt and oil, and stir vigorously with a spoon until thoroughly combined. Taste a little and add more salt if necessary.

Pour into a clean jam jar with a lid and store in the fridge for several days or until needed.

TUSCAN BASIL SAUCE
Pesto toscano

The vibrant flavours of Tuscany, including basil, Pecorino and walnuts, combine to make a perfect sauce for a quick pasta lunch.

Makes a quantity to fit into a clean, empty jam jar:
20g pine nuts
20g walnut pieces
2 large handfuls of basil leaves, roughly chopped
½ a clove of garlic, very finely chopped
flaky sea salt
black pepper
130ml extra virgin olive oil, maybe more
30g grated Parmesan
20g grated Pecorino

Toast the pine nuts and walnuts by dry-frying them in a large, heavy pan over a high heat for no more than 2 minutes. They will be ready when you can smell them in the air and they are just starting to colour. Set aside and allow them to cool.

Roughly chop the basil leaves and place in a blender. Chop the cooled nuts and add them too, along with the garlic, a pinch of salt and a twist of black pepper. Pour in the olive oil, turn on the blender and pulse. The pesto should turn into a gloopy, liquid paste. If it doesn't, turn off the blender, shake the contents and try again. If it needs help, add a little more olive oil. When the liquid is turning, add the Parmesan and the Pecorino until your pesto is smooth and consistent.

Pour and encourage into a clean jam jar with a lid, and store in the fridge for several days or until needed.

TUSCAN TOMATO SAUCE
Salsa di pomodoro toscana

A simple sauce with a multitude of uses. What makes it particularly Tuscan is the use of Costoluto tomatoes, the flat, ribbed variety. Use ripe San Marzano or beef tomatoes if you can't get the Tuscan variety.

Makes 1 litre:
800g Costoluto tomatoes
extra virgin olive oil
flaky sea salt
black pepper
2 tablespoons tomato purée
1 large onion, finely chopped
1 large carrot, peeled and finely chopped
1 celery stalk, finely chopped
1 clove of garlic, finely chopped
1 bay leaf

Put the tomatoes into a large bowl and cover with boiling water directly from the kettle. Leave for a few minutes, then carefully remove. When they are cool enough to handle, but still hot, make a shallow cut with a sharp knife all around the perimeter and peel off the skin. Cut the tomatoes into small chunks, around 3cm, discarding the stalk ends.

Place a large frying pan over a medium heat with a little olive oil and gently fry the skinless tomato pieces. Add a few pinches of salt and black pepper, and the tomato purée. Cook for around 5 minutes until the edges are starting to disintegrate, then add enough water to cover. Bring to the boil, then reduce to a simmer for 5 minutes.

Heat a good few glugs of olive oil in a large saucepan over a medium heat. Sauté the onion, carrot, celery and garlic for 10 minutes until soft and translucent, being careful not to brown. Add the contents of the frying pan to the saucepan and stir well. Drop in the bay leaf, turn the heat to low, cover and simmer for 45 minutes, stirring occasionally. You may need to add a splash or two of water if the sauce is too dry. Remove from the heat and allow to stand for 10 minutes to cool.

Taste and add more salt if necessary, remove the bay leaf and transfer to a blender. Pulse for 1 minute until smooth, pour into a large clean lidded jar (or jars) and store in the fridge for several days or until needed.

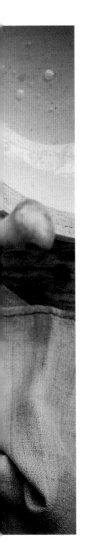

ANCHOVY DRESSING
Condimento di acciughe

*Used principally for the puntarelle recipe on page 115, but great with chicory leaves
or as a dip for crunchy fresh vegetables like celery, carrots and radishes.*

Enough for a couple of salads:
2 × 50g tins of anchovies
1 clove of garlic, peeled
juice of 1 lemon
extra virgin olive oil

Put the anchovies, including the oil from the tin, into a large pestle and mortar with
the garlic. Mash together thoroughly to create a paste. Transfer to a mixing bowl and
loosen the paste with the lemon juice. Stir to combine and, while continuing to stir,
drizzle olive oil slowly until the mixture resembles a loose dressing.

Transfer to a clean jam jar with a lid and keep in the fridge for several days or
until needed.

TARRAGON DRESSING
Condimento di dragoncello

This is the dressing we use on our house salad. It goes exceptionally well with any green leaf or even with chopped cucumbers.

Makes a quantity to fit into a clean, empty jam jar:
100ml extra virgin olive oil
30ml red wine vinegar
3 heaped teaspoons Dijon mustard
3 heaped teaspoons dried tarragon
flaky sea salt
black pepper
caster sugar

Take a clean jam jar with a tight-fitting lid and put in the olive oil, vinegar, mustard, tarragon, a good pinch of salt, a good twist of pepper and a couple of pinches of caster sugar. Shake vigorously until combined and emulsified.

SIMPLE BREAD DOUGH
Pasta di pane

Makes six to eight little bar pizzas (pages 52–61)
Makes roughly 16 coccoli *(page 37)*
500g '00' flour, and more for dusting
2 teaspoons fine salt
7g instant dried yeast
extra virgin olive oil

Put the flour into a large mixing bowl and stir in the salt and the yeast. Add a tablespoon of olive oil and about 200ml of warm water from a measuring jug of 500ml. Using your hands, combine the flour and warm water to create a soft dough, adding more warm water, little by little, kneading the whole time. You may not need to use all the remaining warm water, but just make sure the dough doesn't become too wet. When you have a smooth, firm dough, transfer it on to a floured work surface and knead for a further 10 minutes, pulling back and pushing forward.

When you prod the dough it should spring back a little. Roll it into a ball, put it into a large bowl, cover it with a damp tea towel or oiled clingfilm and leave it in a warm place for about 2 hours until it has doubled in size.

When you are ready to use the dough, remove it, knock it back down to size on a freshly floured work surface, then divide it into the size you need for pizzas or *coccoli*. Give another little dusting of flour and a further 20-minute rest.

SIMPLE PASTA DOUGH
Impasto per pasta

This is the simplest and most universal egg pasta recipe I know. It's perfect for a multitude of uses, making little gnocchi shapes by rolling it into a long, thin sausage, chopping it into 3cm lozenges and pushing them down with the back of a fork, or flattening it with a rolling pin and making hand-cut tagliatelle. No need for a pasta machine.

Makes 400g pasta:
2 large free-range eggs
3 free-range egg yolks
350g '00' flour

Place the eggs and yolks in a bowl and lightly whisk them together.

Empty the flour on to a clean work surface and make a well in the middle, like the vent of a volcano. Put the whisked eggs and yolks into the centre and carefully bring the sides into the middle. Mix gently to create a dough. Knead until smooth. Wrap in clingfilm and allow it to rest for 45 minutes before using. Alternatively place, wrapped, in the fridge until you need it, but allow it 45 minutes to come to room temperature before unwrapping.

TUSCAN BREAD
Pane toscana

I didn't understand Tuscan bread at first. Dry, pale and unsalted, it used to taste unfinished and mean-spirited. Then I realised what I was doing wrong. You don't eat this bread on its own, you use it to accompany the strong flavours of rich stews and sauces, cured meats and salty cheeses, or as an ingredient in those classic Tuscan recipes that call for 'stale' bread. The absence of salt also greatly improves the ability of the yeast to rise. Make the starter (biga) the day before for best results.

Makes one large loaf:
500g '00' flour, and more for dusting
7g instant dried yeast
oil, for greasing

To make the *biga*, place 4 heaped tablespoons of the flour into a bowl with the instant yeast and add 4 tablespoons of warm water. Mix into a dough, cover and leave in a warm place overnight or for at least 3–4 hours.

Next day (or 3–4 hours) later, the *biga* will have doubled or perhaps tripled in size. Put the rest of the flour – there will be around 420g remaining – into a large mixing bowl and combine the *biga* with the flour. Fill a measuring jug with 300ml of warm water and slowly pour, a little at a time, into the bowl with one hand while stirring with the other. You may not need all the water, so assess as you go. Use a little flour if it's too wet or a little more warm water if too dry.

Turn the dough on to a lightly floured surface and knead for 10–12 minutes, until soft and easy to form into a ball. Place back into the mixing bowl, cover with clingfilm or a damp cloth, and leave in a warm place for at least 1 hour, preferably 2.

When the dough has doubled in size, turn it back out on to a lightly floured work surface and form it into a classic loaf shape, rounded and twice as long as it is wide. Lightly oil a large baking sheet and carefully place the dough in the centre. Pinch a ridge all along the middle, then cover with a damp cloth and leave alone for its final prove – around 45 minutes.

Preheat the oven to 200°C.

Using a sharp knife or a bread razor, make shallow diagonal incisions across the ridge and bake for 15 minutes, then reduce the oven to 180°C for a further 30 minutes, but check on it towards the end to make sure it's not looking too dark. It should be a pale but slightly golden colour. Remove and cool on a rack.

ROSEMARY & OLIVE OIL BREAD
Focaccia

A complete contrast to the previous austere recipe, focaccia *is moist, salty, fragrant and unctuously textured. It's a meal in itself, the only bread I know that can sometimes dribble down your chin.*

Makes one large focaccia:
500g '00' flour
1 heaped teaspoon fine salt
7g instant dried yeast
100ml extra virgin olive oil
1 heaped teaspoon flaky sea salt
a handful of rosemary leaves

Put the flour and fine salt into a large mixing bowl and stir with a wooden spoon to combine. Add the yeast but don't stir. Make a well in the middle. Fill a measuring jug with 400ml of warm water.

Pour about one third of the olive oil into the bowl and begin to mix with the flour, using the wooden spoon. Now pour in the warm water, slowly, with one hand while mixing with your other hand. You may not need all the water, so continue to mix and assess until the dough looks formed but slightly sticky. Empty the dough on to a lightly floured surface and knead for 10–12 minutes until smooth and springy. Place back in the cleaned and dried mixing bowl, cover with clingfilm or a damp cloth, and leave in a warm place until doubled in size – around 1½–2 hours.

Use a little of the oil to grease a large baking sheet. Remove the enlarged dough from the bowl, stretch it on a lightly floured surface to roughly the same size and shape as the baking sheet, then transfer it. Cover with a damp cloth and leave in a warm place for its second prove, around 45 minutes. At the 40-minute mark, preheat the oven to 200°C.

Uncover the dough on the tray, press your finger in several times to create about 20 dimples, then pour over one half of the remaining oil and scatter the sea salt flakes evenly. Push the rosemary leaves vertically into the dimples. Sprinkle with a little water and place the tray in the oven. Bake for 20–25 minutes.

Remove from the oven and drizzle over the remaining olive oil. Cut into rectangles and eat while still warm, or allow to cool for use later.

DO

The philosophy and spirit of simplicity in traditional Italian regional cooking permeates through to *dolci*, too, and you will find that less is more on the dessert trolley just as it is in the *trattoria* kitchen. All the family-favourite cakes and tarts from *nonna's* repertoire are held up as the gold standard in Florence's restaurants, supplemented with dishes of fresh fruit prepared simply and the occasional biscuit or meringue cookie. I have also noted that there is a lot of booze in evidence at the sweet end of the menu, as it seems Florentines believe there's nothing that can't be improved by the addition of alcohol.

As in all the Italian regions, sweet dishes are quite often connected with a particular festival or saint. You will find their availability limited because of this tradition, appearing just a few days before and a few days after the event or religious occasion that gives the dish significance. I suppose the equivalent in the UK might be chocolate eggs at Easter, mince pies at Christmas and pancakes on Shrove Tuesday. It would be strange indeed to see any of these at other times of the year, just as it would in Florence to see rice fritters outside the month of March, for example.

Many of the *dolci* that follow are very adaptable, as they are in Tuscany, to other times of the day; they're not just for the end of a meal. You might want to consider enjoying them with a late morning coffee or an afternoon *aperitivo*. I certainly do, and it makes me feel that I'm eating more like an Italian.

APPLE TART
Torta di mele

Our apple tart sometimes surprises people because it doesn't use pastry. Instead, the lining of butter and caramelised apples creates a subtle crust with a dark, golden brown colour. Without pastry, the apples are left to their own devices to create all the flavour, leaving a decidedly fruity tart.

Makes one large tart:
4 apples, any sweet, crisp variety
2 large free-range eggs
200g caster sugar
1 teaspoon vanilla extract
70g plain flour
1 heaped teaspoon baking powder
a pinch of salt
65ml milk
100g butter, very soft, plus a small knob for lining
1 tablespoon icing sugar, for dusting

Butter a cake tin and line it with greaseproof paper. Peel and core the apples, halve and slice thinly. Preheat the oven to 200°C.

Put the eggs, sugar and vanilla extract into a large bowl and whisk until doubled in size. Add the flour, baking powder and salt and combine together. While still whisking, pour in the milk and add the softened butter until smooth and consistent.

Put the sliced apples into the mix and carefully coat them all thoroughly. Layer the apples flat in circles, starting from the edge and working inwards. Pour a thin layer of the remaining mixture on top.

Place in the oven and cook for 10 minutes, then turn the temperature down to 180°C for 40 minutes. Remove the golden brown tart and allow to cool in the tin for at least 30 minutes before transferring to a large serving plate. Dust the top with the icing sugar, shaken through a small sieve from a height.

Serve at room temperature in slices, perhaps with a scoop of vanilla ice cream, but it's also delicious on its own, with coffee or even for breakfast.

HAZELNUT MERINGUE COOKIES
Brutti ma buoni

As the Italian name suggests, these cookies are misshapen and 'ugly' but they taste 'good'. The trick when making them is to allow the raw meringue cookie mixture to fall haphazardly on to the baking sheet so that the results are wonky and vary in size and shape. Do not be tempted to form them, otherwise they won't be ugly enough.

For about 24 to 30 cookies:
5 large free-range egg whites
1 scant teaspoon vanilla extract
200g caster sugar
300g ground hazelnuts

In a very large mixing bowl, whisk the egg whites and vanilla extract until you see that the mixture is just starting to thicken. Add one third of the caster sugar and continue to whisk for a few minutes. Add another third and continue whisking until the eggs are forming peaks. At this stage, add the final third of sugar and keep whisking until the peaks are stiff and the mixture resembles meringue.

Place the ground hazelnuts in a separate large bowl and transfer one third of the meringue, stirring until you have a consistent paste combining everything. Now add the rest of the meringue and carefully fold to incorporate. Don't stir, but rather fold the mixture over itself to avoid knocking too much air out. Preheat the oven to 160°C.

Line two baking sheets with greaseproof paper. Using a tablespoon, dollop the hazelnut meringue on to the sheets, pushing the mixture off the spoon with your finger. Remember, rough and uneven is the order of the day, not neat and formed.

Bake for about 30 minutes and then check on them. They should be golden brown. Leave in the oven for a little longer if they're looking too pale, but don't let them turn brown either.

Remove, allow to cool completely, and eat them on their own with coffee or with vanilla ice cream as a dessert.

TIRAMISU
Tiramisù

Probably the most famous of all Italian desserts, tiramisù *was only a recent addition to the canon. Most agree it was invented at Le Becchiere restaurant in Treviso by Ado Campeol and his wife Alba di Pillo in the 1970s. But Tuscans claim the recipe (if not the name) was their creation as early as the seventeenth century in Siena, when the dish was served to Grand Duke Cosimo III. You need to make the* tiramisù *at least 4 hours before you want to serve it.*

For about 8 portions:
500ml strong coffee
50ml brandy
4 large free-range eggs
150g caster sugar
10ml Marsala
500g mascarpone
a packet of Savoiardi sponge fingers
cocoa powder, for dusting

First make your coffee, using a strong espresso variety in a large stove-top Bialetti Moka coffee maker (other brands are available). Leave it to cool in a large jug, adding the brandy and 100ml of cold water.

Separate the eggs, placing the yolks in one large mixing bowl and the whites in a separate large mixing bowl. Whisk the egg whites vigorously until they start to stiffen. Add half the sugar and continue to whisk energetically until the mix is firm but still glossy.

Clean the whisk and do the same to the yolks, adding the rest of the sugar when the volume starts to increase. Continue whisking until the yolks have doubled in size. Add the Marsala and whisk for another 2–3 minutes. Add half the mascarpone, whisk for 2 minutes, then add the other half and whisk for 2 minutes more until firm.

Using a wooden spoon, gently and slowly fold the egg whites into the yolks without beating or stirring. A folding action from bottom to top and from the sides to the centre is very important so as not to overwork the mixture.

Place a large, high-sided ceramic or glass tray (around 30 × 20cm) on your work surface and begin to dip the sponge fingers into the cold coffee mixture, no more than 3 seconds: they must not disintegrate. Lay the soaked sponge fingers in a single layer on the bottom of the tray. Cover generously with the egg mixture, around 2cm. Do the same again with another layer of sponge fingers and then top those with a final layer of the remaining egg mix. Don't worry if you haven't used all the sponge fingers from a single packet – you can keep them until next time. Finally, dust a liberal layer of cocoa powder on top, completely covering the *tiramisù*, and place the tray in the fridge for at least 4 hours.

Cut the *tiramisù* into large squares and serve on individual plates.

MOIST ALMOND BISCUITS
Ricciarelli

These gorgeous, soft biscuits appear in pasticcerie and bakeries in Florence at Christmas time. They are sometimes presented on rice paper, and although they vary in size from one place to the next, they are always oval with a distinctive dimple in the centre. They are served completely smothered in icing sugar and bring to mind little snowscapes.

For about 20 to 24 biscuits:
3 large free-range egg whites
120g icing sugar
300g ground almonds
zest of 1 orange
280g caster sugar
a knob of butter

Place the egg whites in a large mixing bowl and whisk until they start to stiffen. Add about half the icing sugar and continue to whisk until the mixture resembles a paste. Stir in the ground almonds, orange zest and the caster sugar, combining thoroughly.

Preheat the oven to 180°C.

Put half the remaining icing sugar on a plate and grease two baking sheets with the butter. Using a tablespoon, drop a heaped dollop of the mixture, one at a time, on to the sugared plate. Form the dollops into an oval shape and place them on the greased trays. Gently press an icing-sugared thumb into the centre of each to create a shallow dimple.

Bake for around 20 minutes, but check at 15 minutes. They should look golden and should be beginning to crack. Remove from the oven and totally cover with the remaining icing sugar, distributed at a height from a fine sieve.

Leave to cool for 30 minutes, after which they will be ready to eat. They are perfect with Vin Santo.

SWEET PASTRY 'RAGS'
Cenci

Every Italian region and most major cities celebrate Shrove Tuesday with their own version of Carnevale. *In Venice it's a very big deal and lasts for a few weeks; in Florence it's usually a couple of days either side of* Martedì grasso. *They all have some sort of sweet, fried batter or pastry. Cenci are the Florentine version, translated as 'rags' for obvious visual reasons.*

Makes about 24 to 30:
300g plain flour, and more for dusting
2 large free-range eggs, lightly whisked
50g very soft butter
125ml Vin Santo
30g caster sugar
a pinch of salt
1 teaspoon baking powder
zest of 1 lemon
1 litre sunflower oil, for frying
2 tablespoons icing sugar

Put the flour into a very large mixing bowl and make a well. Add the eggs, butter, Vin Santo, caster sugar, salt, baking powder and lemon zest and mix together with a wooden spoon. Turn out on to a lightly floured surface and knead for a few minutes until you have a soft, smooth dough. Cover and leave for 30 minutes.

Roll out the dough using a rolling pin and try to get it as thin as possible, the same thickness as a sheet of lasagne. Using a notched pasta wheel, cut into strips about 10 × 5cm – slightly larger than a business card.

Heat the oil in a large saucepan to around 180°C, so that a small cube of bread turns brown in 20 seconds. Introduce the *cenci* to the hot oil, probably in batches, until they turn golden brown, around 2 minutes. They will twist and spiral into lovely shapes (sometimes referred to as *farfalle* – butterflies).

Remove with a slotted spoon and drain on kitchen paper. Transfer to a large serving plate and sprinkle very generously with the icing sugar, distributed from a height using a fine sieve.

APPLE FRITTERS
Frittelle di mele

This is a fun preparation for apples, making them look a bit like doughnuts and frying them in batter for a crispy, sweet treat. It's the sort of dessert best served on a large platter and offered around the table rather than presenting on individual plates. The variety of apple isn't too important, but they work best with sweet, crisp varieties as there's no sugar in the recipe, just a sprinkling before serving while they're still hot.

For about 20 to 24 fritters:
100g plain flour
1 large free-range egg
275ml whole milk
a pinch of salt
4 apples
1 litre sunflower oil, for frying
caster sugar

In a large mixing bowl, combine the flour, egg, milk and salt and beat with a wooden spoon into a smooth batter. This will be slightly thicker than pancake batter. Put into the fridge for 30 minutes.

Core the apples using a steel corer so that each has a neat hole through the centre. Slice into 1cm rings – there should be around 6 rings per apple.

Heat the oil in a large saucepan to 170°C, or when a cube of bread turns brown in about 30 seconds. Dip the apple rings into the batter and fry for around 3 minutes until golden and crisp. Drain on kitchen paper, transfer to a large platter and sprinkle liberally with caster sugar. Serve immediately, maybe with a small glass of Vecchia Romagna Italian brandy.

SWEET GRAPE BREAD CAKE
Schiacciata con l'uva

When grapes are harvested in autumn, most are used for winemaking, some are eaten as they are, but many of the smaller, dark, sweet varieties appear in this traditional September cake. Don't be tempted to use seedless supermarket grapes – they're too big and watery and lack flavour. Find small, black, seeded grapes around the same size as plump blueberries.

For one large, rectangular cake:
650g sweet black seeded grapes
the dough recipe on page 229
flour, for dusting
150g caster sugar
a handful of rosemary leaves
extra virgin olive oil

Grease a large baking sheet (about 40 × 30cm) with a little olive oil.

Wash the grapes, remove the stalks and dry thoroughly. Set aside.

Place the rested dough on a lightly floured work surface and divide into two halves. Roll each flat with a floured rolling pin, then use your hands to stretch into two rough rectangles roughly the same size and shape as the baking sheet. Lay one sheet of dough on the tray and pull the sides slightly over the edge of the tray if it's flat, or push the edges up the sides if it has a higher lip.

Distribute half the grapes evenly over the dough, pressing gently with your thumb. Squash a few of them to make them burst. Scatter over half the sugar, half the rosemary, and liberally drizzle with olive oil. Lay the next sheet of dough on top and do exactly the same with the remaining grapes, sugar and rosemary. Drizzle again with olive oil.

Allow the cake to rest somewhere warm for 20–30 minutes, and preheat the oven to 200°C.

Bake for 30 minutes until golden brown. Remove from the oven and serve hot in square slices. It's also delicious warm or at room temperature.

ALMOND & BLOOD ORANGE TART
Torta di mandorle e arancia rossa

In the winter and spring, when blood oranges are in season, I find them hard to resist. It's not just the striking colour that sometimes startles as you peel back the skin, but the juice and flesh have a compelling sweetness and the zest a tangy bitterness which makes common and navel oranges pale in comparison. Literally.

Makes one cake, 8 portions:
2 large free-range eggs
120g caster sugar
70g plain flour
120g very soft butter, and more for greasing
120g ground almonds
1 teaspoon baking powder
juice of 2 blood oranges
zest of 2 blood oranges
1 tablespoon icing sugar

Separate the eggs, placing the whites in a large mixing bowl and the yolks in a cup. Whisk the egg whites vigorously until soft peaks form and set aside. Preheat the oven to 180°C.

In a separate large mixing bowl, mix the yolks and sugar together with a wooden spoon until firm and creamy. Add the flour, 100g of the butter, the ground almonds and baking powder and stir to combine, then add the orange juice and three-quarters of the zest and mix again to form a loose cake mix. Carefully fold in the whipped egg whites.

Use the remaining butter to grease an 18/20cm cake tin with a removable base, covering the bottom and the sides. Spoon in the batter and scatter over the remaining zest.

Bake for 35–40 minutes until golden, and test with a skewer – it should come out dry. Bake for a little longer if not.

Remove and allow to stand for 5 minutes before removing from the tin. Transfer to a large plate and sprinkle the icing sugar at height from a fine sieve. Serve slices on their own with coffee or on separate plates, perhaps with a dollop of mascarpone cream and a small glass of Grand Marnier.

RICE FRITTERS
Frittelle di riso

Rice frittelle *are served in Florence on 19 March for the feast of St Giovanni. Fittingly he is the patron saint of friers. The date also happens to be Father's Day in Italy – Festa del Papà. There are many recipe variations and the method varies greatly, too. This one is fairly authentic, but with the addition of raisins after I tried it this way in Borgo San Lorenzo a few years ago.*

Makes about 40 frittelle:
50g raisins
500ml whole milk
100g pudding rice
zest of 1 lemon
caster sugar
3 medium free-range eggs
50g plain flour
1 teaspoon baking powder
a pinch of salt
25ml rum
1 litre sunflower oil, for frying

Soak the raisins in warm water for 30 minutes, drain, and rest on kitchen paper to dry.

Put the milk into a large saucepan and add the rice. Gently bring to the boil over a medium heat and when the milk starts to rise, turn down to a simmer. Cook for about 40 minutes, stirring frequently to prevent the rice sticking to the bottom of the pan and watching always to prevent it overflowing. You may need to add a little more milk if it looks like it has been absorbed too quickly. After 40 minutes, test a grain or two – it should be soft and creamy. Add the lemon zest and 4 tablespoons of caster sugar, stir, and remove from the heat. Allow it to cool.

Add the eggs, flour, baking powder and a pinch of salt and stir. Now add the rum and raisins and stir again. Leave in a warm place for 1 hour.

Heat the oil in a large, wide pan to 170°C, or when a cube of bread turns brown in 30 seconds.

Using a dessertspoon, drop dollops of the batter into the oil, turning if necessary, and remove to kitchen paper with a slotted spoon when they are golden brown. You will need to do this in batches. Cover a wide plate with a generous amount of caster sugar and roll the fritters in it, then transfer to a large serving plate. Sprinkle even more sugar on to the plate and eat immediately.

LEMON & VODKA SMOOTHIE
Sgroppino

You could quite justifiably enjoy a sgroppino on its own on a hot afternoon as a cooling aperitivo, but it is mostly served after a meal as a clean and zingy dessert. In restaurants and trattorie you will often see it made tableside by the waiter. It is important that the ingredients are incorporated fully, resulting in a pure white foam rather than a sad glass of supercharged prosecco with a floating iceberg of sorbet.

For four:
400g lemon sorbet
100ml vodka
200ml prosecco

Make sure the prosecco is in the fridge and the bottle of vodka is in the freezer at least 1½ hours before you make these. I put the wine glasses in the freezer, too, particularly on a warm day.

Put the sorbet, vodka and prosecco into a large bowl. Using a stick blender or a whisk, completely combine everything to create a smooth, creamy, foamy consistency. Transfer to a large jug and pour into four chilled wine glasses. Serve with a teaspoon although it is perfectly acceptable to drink straight from the glass.

(Alternative: use Campari instead of vodka for a delightfully bitter *aperitivo* or *digestivo*.)

PISTACHIO BISCUITS
Cantuccini

Cantuccini are the quintessential Italian biscuit. They are easy to make and have a long shelf-life if kept in an airtight Tupperware container. As well as the serving suggestions below, they are also perfect with a scoop of ice cream or as an accompaniment to the sgroppino recipe on the previous pages.

Makes about 30 biscuits:
3 large free-range eggs
400g caster sugar
seeds from 1 vanilla pod
1 heaped teaspoon sesame seeds
1 teaspoon fennel seeds
150g pistachios
100g walnut pieces
100g almonds
500g '00' flour
2 teaspoons baking powder
300ml sunflower oil
a knob of butter
Vin Santo, for serving

Beat the eggs, sugar and all the seeds together in a large mixing bowl with a wooden spoon.

Chop the nuts roughly or bash in a pestle and mortar.

Slowly add the flour, the baking powder and the oil and continue to combine with your spoon. Add the nuts and mix thoroughly. Place in the fridge and leave overnight.

The following day, grease two baking sheets with the butter and line with greaseproof paper. Preheat the oven to 180°C. Divide the mixture into two and create two long, squat loaves.

Bake for 25–30 minutes. Remove from the oven and when cool enough to handle but still slightly yielding, slice into 2cm lozenges. Lay the slices on their side on a wire rack and place back in the oven at 120°C for 10 minutes, or until golden.

Traditionally served with Vin Santo for dipping, but they are also delicious with a coffee.

FROZEN GRAPES, GRAPPA & DARK CHOCOLATE

Uva surgelata, grappa e cioccolato fondente

This is a cunning little combination of flavours, giving the chocolate hit I always crave after a meal, along with a small, strong glass of grappa. The surprise is that the grapes turn into little globes of sorbet in the freezer.

For four:
500g small, seedless, sweet grapes
a 100g bar of excellent dark chocolate, 70% cocoa
good grappa

Place the grapes in the freezer for 2 hours.

Break the chocolate bar into small, uneven chunks, the size of large postage stamps, and set aside somewhere cool (but not the fridge).

After 2 hours, divide the frozen grapes equally between four plates. Do the same with the chocolate. Pour the grappa into small glasses and place one on each plate with a teaspoon. Serve to your guests with the instruction to do what they like with the three elements. Dip the chocolate, dip the grapes, whatever.

COFFEE-DRENCHED ICE CREAM WITH VECCHIA ROMAGNA
Affogato corretto

I've said it before and I'll say it again: Italian cooking uses a lot of booze. I think it's a healthier way to approach alcohol compared to other cultures where it's seen as a separate entity. In Italy it is an essential part of the dining experience and makes its way into many traditional dishes. There is another national idiosyncrasy which I love and that is the notion of 'correcting' a variety of offerings by adding alcohol. In the winter months, you will often hear senior citizens ordering caffè corretto *— an espresso corrected with a tot of grappa. This recipe has also been 'corrected'.*

For four:
4 espressos
4 scoops of vanilla ice cream
100ml Vecchia Romagna Italian brandy

Take 12 small glasses — Duralex tumblers are perfect — and arrange on four plates.

Make a large Moka stove-top coffee maker of espresso-grade coffee. While it's bubbling away, put a scoop of ice cream into one of the glasses on each plate. Pour 25ml of Vecchia Romagna into the second glass on each plate. Finally, pour the freshly made coffee into the third glass. Serve with a teaspoon each and instruct your guests to add the coffee to the ice cream and then pour over the Vecchia Romagna.

FLORENTINES
Biscotti con mandorle, nocciole, zenzero e cioccolato

Here's a slight anomaly. Although I have always known these cookies as Florentines, there doesn't seem to be an equivalent in Italian for the name. They are certainly not called Fiorentine, *which would have made sense. They are also, strictly speaking, not* biscotti, *as that word relates to biscuits that are cooked twice. I've swapped the traditional glacé cherries for ginger, as I like the mildly spicy result.*

Makes about 18:
75g hazelnuts
75g flaked almonds
75g glacé ginger
30g butter, plus a knob for greasing
50g caster sugar
50g golden syrup
50g plain flour
20g double cream
200g dark chocolate, 70% cocoa

Roughly chop the hazelnuts and almond flakes or bash them in a pestle and mortar. Chop the glacé ginger. Set aside.

Grease three baking sheets with the knob of butter and line with greaseproof paper. Preheat the oven to 180°C.

Place the butter, sugar and golden syrup in a saucepan and heat slowly until the butter has melted and the sugar has dissolved. Take off the heat and stir in the flour, nuts, glacé ginger and double cream with a wooden spoon until fully combined.

Using a dessertspoon, place heaped dollops of the mixture on the three baking sheets, leaving space between them to spread, 6 dollops per tray. Bake for 10 minutes until golden brown. Remove and allow to cool.

Break the chocolate into pieces and place in a heatproof Pyrex bowl over a saucepan of simmering water. Make sure the water doesn't touch the bowl. When the chocolate has melted, shut off the heat, dip each Florentine into the melted chocolate to coat half only, generously. Don't worry about being neat and precise – mine never are, I prefer the wonky presentation with differing chocolate levels and shapes. Return the dipped Florentines to the greaseproof paper until fully hardened. You may want to put them into the fridge for 30 minutes to speed up the process, but eat them at room temperature.

STRAWBERRIES IN THEIR OWN SAUCE
Fragole in salsa di fragole

In the summer months, the venerable Florentine trattoria Sostanza (page 303) has a very simple dolci menu which usually consists of fresh raspberries or strawberries dusted with icing sugar. As you might imagine, the fruit is ripe, deeply coloured and packed with natural sugars. Sometimes, in colder climes, this isn't always the case. Strawberries in particular can be a bit underwhelming when I buy them in the UK. The tell-tale sign is a white centre when sliced, rather than a uniform deep red. This recipe addresses that problem.

For four:
1 lemon
a handful of fresh mint leaves
1kg ripe strawberries
a large knob of butter
100g caster sugar
1 heaped tablespoon icing sugar

Zest the lemon, then juice just half of it, removing any pips. Shred the mint leaves with a sharp knife. Set all aside.

Destalk and hull all the strawberries and slice them in half lengthways.

Melt the butter in a saucepan and add the caster sugar, lemon juice and zest. Gently stir with a wooden spoon over a low heat until the sugar has dissolved and add one quarter of the strawberries. Continue to simmer and stir for 10 minutes, until the strawberries have started to collapse. You can encourage this by squashing them with the back of the spoon. Add a splash of water if it's looking too dry. Remove from the heat and allow to cool. When cooled, strain through a sieve into a pouring jug, pressing the solids down with the back of the spoon to get all the juice.

Divide the remaining strawberries between four plates, pour over the sauce and scatter over the shredded mint. Finally, distribute the icing sugar at a height from a fine sieve.

PECORINO WITH MELTED SUGAR
Pecorino con zucchero bruciato

One night at Trattoria Cammillo in Oltrarno (page 302) I had eaten so much that I decided to skip dessert. Chiara, the owner, was having none of this nonsense and proceeded to send two wonderful dishes — baked peaches and a honey and lemon cake I think — because she insisted we had to try them. While we were enjoying the dolci *and Chiara's generosity I noticed a waiter with a blowtorch a few tables away. 'What's that?' I asked. 'Pecorino brûlée,' replied Chiara, 'and I'm sending you one right now.' I have no idea how I found room for more food, but the melted sugar, the slightly softened Pecorino, the salty sweetness and the crunch were too much. It was a sensation, so I absolutely had to include a recipe here to thank Chiara.*

Needless to say, you need a small catering blowtorch to make this.

For four:
250g Pecorino Romano
180g golden caster sugar

Slice the Pecorino into 12 triangles around 1cm thick. Lay the slices on a baking sheet and distribute roughly 1 tablespoon of caster sugar on to the flat surface of each slice.

With the blowtorch on a low flame (you don't want to risk blowing off the sugar with too much force), gently melt the sugar until golden brown / nutty brown but not too dark. Transfer 3 slices on to each of four plates and serve immediately.

BEVA

At BRUTTO we serve classic cocktails along with a few of our home-grown originals. The demand for our House Negroni, a reasonably faithful rendering of the traditional combination of gin, Campari and sweet vermouth, but using an infused gin-based *amaro* called Nostrano, was stratospheric. This may be because we undercut the standard price of Negronis in London by 65%. We will continue to do this. It makes BRUTTO a destination for discerning drinkers at our antique marble-topped bar as well as for fans of Florentine cooking. Creating an atmosphere is as important as serving authentic Tuscan dishes and providing friendly, knowledgeable and convivial service.

When we put together the cocktail list we were inspired by the drinking culture of the students, artists and musicians who frequent Piazza Santo Spirito after dark, but also the elegant international hotel bars in the historic centre of Florence, where white-coated bartenders make Martinis and Daquiris in a manner of which Hemingway would have approved.

LIMONCELLO COLLINS
Limoncello 'Collins'

Quite often at the end of a meal in a traditional Florentine trattoria, *the manager or owner will come to the table offering complementary glasses of limoncello, a rather sweet and sticky lemon liqueur. I have to be honest, it's not my preferred way to end a meal, and I suspect it's code for 'We want your table back for the next sitting.' But as an ingredient it can be very useful to give a sweet but citrusy tang.*

For one:
50ml gin
50ml limoncello
25ml lemon juice
2 teaspoons sugar syrup (page 285)
soda water, to top up
a slice of lemon

Put the gin, limoncello, lemon juice and sugar syrup into a cocktail shaker half-filled with ice. Shake for 10 seconds.

Fill a large tumbler with fresh ice and strain the contents of the shaker into the glass, adding a splash of soda water.

Garnish with the slice of lemon.

BRUTTO NEGRONI
Negroni della casa

*Our Negroni differs slightly from the classic version. We use an infused gin called Nostrano.
It's an* amaro *that was developed and is produced by Luca da Vita, from the celebrated Venetian
restaurant Alle Testiere, and me. We use London dry gin, purple artichokes, wormwood, marsh
samphire, orange, rhubarb root and sea water from the Adriatic. I admit it's not easy to get hold
of at the time of writing but is always available online at www.amaronostrano.com. The other
difference is the use of Select, a milder and more niche* amaro *which is widely available
in specialist Italian delis.*

For one:
25ml Nostrano
25ml Select
25ml Martini Rosso
a slice of orange

Fill a tumbler with ice and pour over the Nostrano, Select and Martini Rosso.
Stir gently for 10 seconds and garnish with the orange slice.

BRUTTO SPRITZ
Spritz della casa

Select was first developed in Venice in 1920, using thirty botanicals including rhubarb root and juniper berries along with citrus and essential oils. Its bold and vibrant colour seems to glow in the glass, and it is always served with an olive.

For one:
50ml Select
75ml prosecco
a splash of soda water (or fizzy mineral water)
1 large, crunchy green olive

Take a large stemmed wine glass and half-fill with ice. Pour over the Select and stir a few times to coat the ice cubes. Add the prosecco and a splash of soda water and stir again. Garnish with the green olive, speared on a long wooden skewer.

GODFATHER SOUR
Amaretto con whisky e limone

Amaretto sometimes gets a bad rap as an overly-sweet digestivo that is considered a bit kitsch. Using it in a sour addresses that problem and makes for a very drinkable classic. The method is a bit involved, but necessary in order to avoid the murkiness that egg white causes in an otherwise clear cocktail if not put through the two stages below.

For one:
50ml decent Scotch whisky
25ml amaretto
25ml lemon juice
1 teaspoon sugar syrup (page 285)
2 teaspoons egg white
a slice of orange

Fill a large tumbler with ice.

Put all the ingredients (except the orange slice) into a cocktail shaker half-filled with ice. Shake vigorously for 10 seconds, then strain into a second, clean shaker. Dry shake for 5 seconds, then pour through a bar strainer into the prepared tumbler.

Garnish with the slice of orange.

MONTENEGRONI
Negroni con Amaro Montenegro

Although distilled originally in 1885 in Bologna, Amaro Montenegro has achieved worldwide appeal as a unique digestivo. *It has a distinct, herby flavour from Mediterranean oregano and marjoram, with spice notes from clove and cinnamon. There's also a background hint of eucalyptus. We use Antica Formula vermouth but you could easily substitute that with a more widely available brand like Martini Rosso. It is a very popular alternative to the classic Negroni at BRUTTO.*

For one:
25ml gin
25ml Amaro Montenegro
25ml Antica Formula vermouth
orange peel

Fill a tumbler with ice. Pour over the gin, Amaro Montenegro and Antica Formula. Stir for a few seconds. Take an orange and, using a potato peeler or very sharp knife, shave off a large, thin piece of peel, taking care not to cut into the pith. Gently twist the peel, face down, over the drink. Wipe the rim of the glass with the peel, then drop it in, face up.

APEROL SOUR
Aperol con gin e limone

Aperol is the sweeter, milder cousin of Campari. It has achieved huge popularity outside of Italy and can be a little cloying to my taste, but in this sour cocktail it provides a refreshing and lighter alternative to traditional whisky. The gin is there to ensure the drink still has a punch, with plenty of acidity from the lemon juice.

For one:
50ml Aperol
25ml gin
2 teaspoons lemon juice
25ml sugar syrup (page 285)
2 teaspoons free-range egg white
lemon peel

Put all the ingredients (except the lemon peel) into a cocktail shaker half-filled with ice and shake vigorously for 10 seconds. Pour through a bar strainer into a chilled coupe glass, making sure to hold back the ice. Using a potato peeler or a very sharp knife, create a long strip of lemon peel and carefully float it on the surface as a garnish.

BOULEVARDIER
Boulevardier

I first had this drink in Harry's Bar in Venice. Although it is often described as a Negroni made with bourbon instead of gin, I think that does it a disservice. It has its own distinct character and personality. In Florence I've only ever seen it served on the rocks, so that's the version we make at BRUTTO, too. It's been around for over ninety years and is probably so-called after the Parisian magazine of the same name.

For one:
35ml bourbon
25ml Campari
25ml sweet vermouth
orange peel
1 Amarena cherry

Fill a large, heavy-bottomed glass with ice. Carefully pour the bourbon, Campari and sweet vermouth over the ice. Stir gently for 10 seconds.

Take a large slice of peel from an orange without any pith and skewer it into the Amarena cherry with a cocktail stick. Place the garnish in the drink.

(In case you are wondering, the glass I have used here is designed by Arnolfo di Cambio and is the one Harrison Ford uses in the film *Blade Runner*.)

MILANO-TORINO
Milano-Torino

A classic, even in the simplest bars and caffès. It's essentially an Americano for people who don't want to dilute their liquor by adding water, offering the two ingredients more space to tingle the tongue. It's sometimes referred to as a Mi-To.

For one:
50ml Campari
50m Martini Rosso
a wedge of orange

Fill a large tumbler with ice. Pour in the Campari and sweet vermouth. Stir for a few seconds. Garnish with a wedge of orange.

ITALIAN OLD FASHIONED
'Old Fashioned' Italiano

I love an Old Fashioned. It's one of the earliest cocktails, dating back to the 1880s, and is often considered in the top five 'essentials' by bartenders around the world. Having said that, I think I might prefer this version. It still has the glorious whisky kick but with all the aromatics that Amaro Montenegro brings.

For one:
orange peel
50ml rye whiskey
25ml Amaro Montenegro
1 teaspoon runny honey
tiniest pinch of salt
3 dashes Peychaud bitters

Set up a large whisky / whiskey glass full of ice. Shave a large piece of orange peel using a potato peeler or a sharp knife. Make sure there is no pith on the back of the skin.

Pour all the liquids with the salt and bitters into a jug full of ice. Stir with a long-handled spoon for around 20 seconds in one direction only. Strain into the prepared glass.

Twist the orange peel gently over the drink to release some of the oil in the skin, wipe it around the rim, and drop it into glass, skin side up.

LEMON DROP
Limoncello con vodka

A refreshing cocktail making use of limoncello in a sophisticated way. The flavours are a little bolder than, say, a sgroppino, which has a similar base ingredient profile, but the sugared rim softens the package and adds a bit of visual fun, too.

For one:
1 tablespoon caster sugar
a lemon wedge
75ml limoncello
50ml vodka
2 teaspoons lemon juice
lemon peel

Start by preparing a traditional small wine glass or coupe. Put the sugar into a saucer. Take the lemon wedge, squeeze it briefly to release the juice, then rub it around the rim of the glass, including about 1cm of the top outer edge. Turn the glass rim around in the sugar to coat it generously.

Put the limoncello, vodka and lemon juice into a cocktail shaker half-filled with ice. Shake enthusiastically for 10 seconds, then strain into the sugared glass.

Shave a long strip of lemon peel with a potato peeler or sharp knife and add to the top of the drink as a garnish.

ITALIAN BRANDY FLIP
Flip con Vecchia Romagna

It seems to be the rule that all the creamy cocktails come out of the liquor cabinet at Christmas, when we crave those warm spices and comforting textures. The brandy flip is a great example of the genre.

For one:
60ml Vecchia Romagna
15ml sugar syrup (page 285)
1 small free-range egg
nutmeg

Half-fill a cocktail shaker with ice and add the Vecchia Romagna, sugar syrup and egg. Shake vigorously for 15 seconds.

Strain through a bar sieve into a chilled Nick & Nora cocktail glass or a similar-sized coupe. Garnish with freshly grated nutmeg.

SUGAR SYRUP
Sciroppo di zucchero

This is a bar essential and is required in many of the preceding drink recipes. It is also very useful when you want to add a little extra sweetness to drinks without worrying about granules, as the sugar is pre-dissolved. It's great to use in coffee, too. The syrup will keep fresh in the fridge for several weeks as long as you store it in a very clean bottle with a lid.

100ml water
200g caster sugar

Put the water and caster sugar into a small saucepan over a medium heat. Watch and stir as the heat rises. It won't take long. When you can see that all the sugar has dissolved, stir a few more times and remove from the heat. Do not let it boil.

Allow to cool completely and pour through a funnel into a clean bottle. Cap the bottle and store in the fridge until needed.

GAZE

To eat and drink well in Florence is actually quite easy if you follow the example of the locals and choose places in which they dine on a regular basis. Meals are rarely taken for special occasions, but rather for day-to-day sustenance and family gatherings. Florentines are far more interested in classic and local cooking than in new twists or cheffy innovation. Here again we find the local philosophy of simplicity and authenticity.

This guide is very subjective and may miss out some of your favourite places if you know Florence well, but these are the restaurants and bars that typify the BRUTTO experience of the city: simple and honest, authentic and traditional. I'm listing them in alphabetical order to avoid any accusation of preference or favouritism. Actually, I love them all equally.

TEER

1 ALLA VECCHIA BETTOLA
2 CASA DEL VINO
3 CIBRÈO
4 I'BRINDELLONE
5 LE VOLPI E L'UVA
6 NERBONE
7 PALAZZO GUADAGNI
8 IL SANTINO
9 TRATTORIA CAMMILLO
10 TRATTORIA MARIO
11 TRATTORIA SABATINO
12 TRATTORIA SOSTANZA

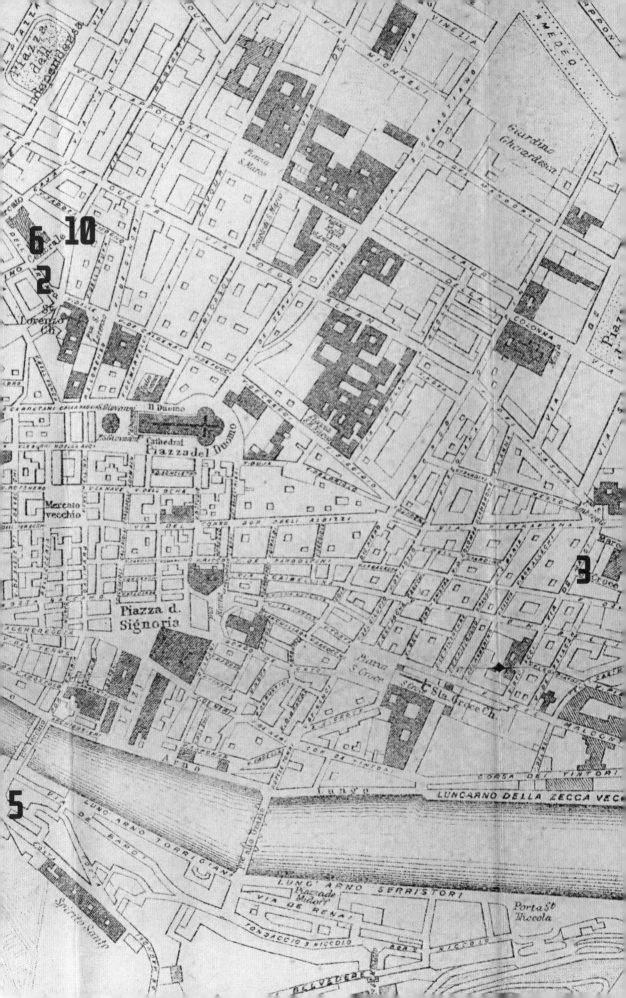

ALLA VECCHIA BETTOLA
Viale Vasco Pratolini 3–7, 50124 Firenze

On the outskirts of Oltrarno in the Bellosguardo district you come to the ugly ring road of Viale Aleardo Aleardi. It's horrible, and it somewhat breaks the spell that Florence casts, but a treat awaits you once you cross the road dodging the speeding traffic. Alla Vecchia Bettola is a favourite destination for workmen, students and locals seeking unpretentious, classic cooking and a surprisingly good house wine which sits on the table in magnums as you arrive. No matter how big or small the group, everyone gets a fiasco magnum (the basket-weave bottles most famous in Chianti) and you pay for what you drink, not for the whole bottle.

Bettola's *crostini neri* are among the best in the city and their most famous dish, penne with vodka and tomato sauce, is a 1980s revival signature dish which we also serve at BRUTTO. (See our recipe on page 79.) The porcelain-tiled walls and varnished hardwood furniture mean that the noise levels are high – it can sometimes seem cacophonous – but its atmosphere is unrivalled in Florence.

CASA DEL VINO
Via dell'Ariento 16, 50123 Firenze

On an early research trip to Florence in 2018 I was staying in a superb hotel called Oltrarno Splendid. At breakfast one morning I bumped into the venerable food and wine writer Bill Knott. He seemed agitated towards the end of our ham, cheese and cake repast (why is the standard Italian hotel breakfast offer always cheese or cake?) and I asked him why. 'Casa del Vino opens at 10 a.m.,' he said. 'I've got to go!' I asked if I could join him and he positively powered through the city to the Central Market like a man with a mission, me trailing behind like a toddler. When we arrived I could see why he was so excited. 'It's my favourite wine bar in the world,' he told me.

Beautifully furnished with antique wooden panelling and Carrara marble, it's an incredibly evocative space with a surprisingly vast array of local wines and a fair smattering of low-intervention, natural varieties by small producers. But what excited me most was the food. The tiny preparation area was brimming with anchovies, roasted vegetables, simple stews, *crostini* and salads. Within just 30 minutes, the space had filled up with wine aficionados, locals and food tourists. I struck up conversations with doctors, politicians, winemakers, and even the chief of police. An essential Florentine experience. (The owners, Gianni and Nicoletta, are the most charming hosts and will help you make the right selection from their carefully chosen list.)

CIBRÈO
Via Andrea del Verrocchio 8, 50122 Firenze

Established in 1979, Cibrèo quickly became one of Florence's most celebrated restaurants and is now something of an institution. The dining room is stunning and the experience feels world-class. Although the menu highlights Tuscan traditions, there are some surprising dishes that tend to follow a nose-to-tail philosophy and, unusually for Florence, there is a fair representation of fish and seafood. Last time I ate there I had a choice of lobster, mussels, oysters and octopus. The dish from which the restaurant takes its name is a challenging concoction that contains chicken testicles, a coxcomb (the floppy red thing on top of a cockerel's head) and the fleshy wattle from under the beak.

Incidentally, close by Cibrèo is the excellent Mercato di Sant'Ambrogio, even more interesting and charming than the famous Mercato Centrale. In addition to the wonderful local produce, there are antiques, budget clothing and all manner of knick-knacks. There is also the super workers' canteen, Trattoria da Rocco, right at the other end of the scale in price point to Cibrèo.

I'BRINDELLONE
Piazza Piattellina 10, 50124 Firenze

Walking west from Piazza Santo Spirito you pass an old-school photo booth on the corner of Via dei Serragli and Via Santa Monaca. Make sure you stop to get a strip of old-school black-and-white passport photos while pulling funny faces. Obligatory. A little further along the street you come to Cappella Brancacci, where the fifteenth-century Renaissance frescos are breathtaking. A few metres more brings you to I'Brindellone. It's a very traditional *trattoria* with no airs or graces, no pretension and loved by all in the neighbourhood. They sometimes get permission to put tables and chairs across the road under large umbrellas and it's a lovely spot for a *fuori* lunch. (Italians never say *al fresco* for outside dining, by the way. It means 'in the cool' or colloquially 'in prison'. They think us English-speakers very odd for using it to mean eating in the open air.) But the inside of I'Brindellone is also very charming and the food is classic home cooking. The taglierini with truffles is excellent and the famous *coccoli* – deep-fried dough balls with prosciutto and *stracchino* (recipe on page 37) – is a must-have.

As with many local *trattorie* the tables are placed very close to each other, so prepare to knock elbows and strike up conversations with your neighbours, but this only adds to the experience in my opinion. The staff are usually quite stretched so can appear brusque but on my second visit they recognised me and brought complementary grappa to the table at the end of the meal.

LE VOLPI E L'UVA
Piazza dei Rossi 1, 50125 Firenze

Sometimes you just need a pit-stop after a morning traipsing the galleries and museums of Florence, and if you find yourself near Ponte Vecchio or the Pitti Palace, Le Volpi e l'Uva (the Foxes & the Grape) is perfectly placed. It's a tiny wine bar with rather good food, too, and I've spent a lot of time there sampling local wines and enjoying their excellent *carne cruda* – Italian steak tartare with anchovies and parsley. The ingredients are always first-rate and although the menu tends to be simple assembly rather than expert cooking, you can eat very well if you fancy converting your drinking session to lunch or dinner. In the spring and summer you can sit outside, but in colder months the stools at the bar are a great place to socialise and chat. The staff are very knowledgeable about the short list and can recommend interesting wines by the glass if you need guidance.

On the way upstairs to the loos you can see the carefully chosen stock through a gated cage and I get the impression they love what they do – always a good sign when choosing where to spend your euros. It's also always a good sign when you see crowds of local art students having fun, arriving on Vespas and kissing each other on both cheeks twice, like a scene from Anthony Minghella's *The Talented Mr Ripley*.

NERBONE
Piazza del Mercato Centrale, 50123 Firenze

The dish most closely associated with Florence is arguably tripe, and the place most closely associated with tripe is Nerbone. It's a market stall, effectively, offering brisket, tongue, *bollito misto* and their world-famous *lampredotto* tripe rolls. The meat is sliced in front of you and you are offered *salsa verde*, *salsa picante* or both. I'd recommend going for both. It's a messy affair, especially as the crusty rolls are dipped in the cooking liquor before being filled. Once your tray is piled high with meaty delights, and perhaps a jug of Sangiovese, you find one of the bench tables opposite and tuck in. (See our version on page 51.)

The queues tend to be quite long at all times, especially lunch hour, so I have got into the habit of going for breakfast. There's nothing quite like spicy, garlicky *lampredotto* at 8 a.m. to start the day. And no one bats an eyelid if you wash it down with a glass of red either. Make sure you check out the hilarious paintings on the back wall of the market stand behind the chef and the servers depicting old regulars (I assume) in various stages of inebriation.

PALAZZO GUADAGNI
Piazza Santo Spirito 9, 50125 Firenze

Guadagni is one of my favourite hotels in Florence. I have had many happy times staying in the piazza-facing bedrooms with large balconies and four-metre-high *trompe-l'œil* painted ceilings. But the reason to go is the rooftop *loggia*, particularly at sunset for a Campari & soda and a snack. The pink canvas sails tied to the columns flutter in the breeze and you feel like you're on a movie set. I have a particular love for swifts – those incredibly fast migrating birds that nest in high buildings' eaves and swoop and screech in the early evening skies catching flying insects – and from the *loggia* at Guadagni you get a wonderful view of them circling high above the piazza (see photo on page 8).

To get access to the roof is quite a challenge the first time. You can either climb the beautiful but seemingly endless stone steps to the top, or you can take a fun ride in the tiny antique elevator which feels cramped even with just two people.

IL SANTINO
Via Santo Spirito 60, 50125 Firenze

I have always been afraid of natural wine. In my (naïve) experience, I used to think it was cloudy, too challenging, looked like chicken stock and tasted like cider. My conversion, like Saul on the road to Damascus, came after a conversation and a long lunch at Il Santino with the art historian Dr Genevieve Verdigel. She patiently took me through some of the principles of natural winemaking and ordered glasses of revelatory wines to make her case. Mine was a swift transformation into Paul and I now laugh at my former ignorance.

Il Santino is a tiny space between Santo Spirito and the Arno with only four tables and a small bar, but it is permanently packed with those who saw the light before I did. There are simple snacks available to supplement the clever selections of low-intervention, small-producer delights and the buzz of conversation is a real bonus, too. It's like a wine-geeks' club.

On a trip with the photographer Jenny Zarins, we experienced a colossal storm (biblical references once again) and I jumped into the street to dance in the rain. Natural wine makes you do crazy things, apparently.

TRATTORIA CAMMILLO
Borgo San Jacopo 57, 50125 Firenze

Cammillo is probably the *trattoria* most closely associated with the local literati, the aesthetes, the bohemians, the intellectuals and the poets. It's at the very centre of the Oltrarno district and tends to get booked up weeks in advance. Having said that, I have walked in without a booking on a very busy night and been seated immediately. This is the sign of a very good restaurant – one that knows how to juggle a table plan with intelligent and instinctive regard for the ebb-and-flow of punters walking in off the street. The food is excellent, obviously, and the daily-printed menu is vast. I have often marvelled at the ability of the relatively small kitchen (usually no more than four chefs and one kitchen porter) to execute over a hundred different dishes with ease, speed and quality. Front-of-house is overseen by owner Chiara, the most charming host, fierce but friendly, eyes everywhere, and a bit of a local celebrity.

Cammillo does its thing in such a slick and elegant way that you always know you are in safe hands. The waiters are all hospitality professionals, not moonlighting actors or models. I can honestly say I have never had a bad meal here nor an experience that wasn't world-class. Order the steak tartare, the excellent homemade pasta or the *vitello tonnato*. Their veal Milanese is particularly good, too (see our version on page 170). And save room for the desserts of simple cakes, fruit and a sensational Pecorino brûlée (see page 265).

TRATTORIA MARIO
Via Rosina 2, 50123 Firenze

I was a late adopter of Mario's after it was introduced to me by a Florentine artist friend. He told me that it was a legendary *trattoria* dating back to the early 1950s near the Central Market and that I had to include it in any guide to the city's best eateries. He wasn't wrong. It's permanently packed and with good reason – the food is just what you want to eat to experience typical Tuscan cooking. The kitchen is located just to the side of the long room and you can see the sauces bubbling away throughout service as they serve up generous portions of pasta, stews, grilled meats and litres of beans. I learnt about a secret dining room downstairs. It's called La Cantina and is favoured by locals who enjoy the cooler cellar temperature and the clandestine atmosphere. You can imagine shady deals taking place with the occasional Mafioso holding court, or career criminals plotting the next great art heist. Or maybe that's just my imagination running away with me.

By the way, Trattoria Mario has very eccentric opening hours which I can never remember – so do check before you turn up. And expect long queues if you haven't booked.

TRATTORIA SABATINO
Via Pisana 2, 50143 Firenze

I was told by many of my local friends in Florence and those in the know that I would be heavily admonished if I included mention of Sabatino in this book. One friend went so far as to tell me to remove an Instagram post in which I recommended it. There is no question that Sabatino is beloved by locals and thought of fondly as a cherished secret. But I love the family that run the kitchen and restaurant, and although they need no more publicity (it is permanently packed) I couldn't *not* include it in a guide to my favourite places.

   Located in the San Frediano district next to a huge section of the original city wall, Sabatino is a *trattoria* and an *alimentari*, meaning that you can pick up a bottle of olive oil, a bar of soap or even a pack of playing cards at the till on the way out. The food is always exceptionally simple but lovingly prepared. The prices are startlingly low, so much so that I don't think you could eat more reasonably if you bought the ingredients from the market yourself and cooked at home instead. Their typed menu is a lesson in functional minimalism and written every day on a 1980s Olivetti Linea 101 electric typewriter. When opening BRUTTO I found the same machine on Italian eBay and followed the Sabatino principle of stark simplicity for our menu, too.

TRATTORIA SOSTANZA
Via del Porcellana 25, 50123 Firenze

Sostanza is an essential Florence experience. Largely unchanged for 150 years, it really does feel like you are stepping back in time when you walk through the door. Located in an unassuming backstreet in a run-down part of the city, it was known for many years as '*Il Troia*', which translates as 'the whore' or 'the trough' or 'the pigsty' depending on which local you talk to. Die-hard fans still refer to it by this nickname.

   There are only six tables and a tiny open kitchen where two chefs manage a simple menu of Florentine classics and a few Sostanza signature dishes. Most famous is the artichoke tart, a delightfully light omelette with fresh artichokes, whipped into a plump disc with the most curious tool – a fork welded on to a longer fork handle. Each chef has his own and they are never swapped. Woe betide the chef who picks up the wrong one. The other must-have menu item is the butter chicken: two moist and very tender breasts so slowly fried in melted butter that they are virtually poached. They are served with a theatrical flourish at the table, still sizzling as they are carefully placed in front of you. And as you would expect of such a venerable Florentine institution, their *bistecca alla Fiorentina* is superb. Cooked over a pile of hot coals that are lit every morning and sustained throughout the day (there is no gas in the kitchen), the steaks are moved up and down a slanted grill depending on the temperature required (see photo on page 139). It's all so basic but it works perfectly. (See our version on page 143.)

INDEX

A

Acciughe, burro e pane 27
Acciughe con scorza d'arancia 47
Affogato corretto 258
almonds: Almond & blood orange tart 249
    Florentines 261
    Moist almond biscuits 241
amaretto: Godfather Sour 275
Amaretto con whisky e limone 275
Amaro Montenegro: Italian Old Fashioned 281
    Montenegroni 276
anchovies: Anchovies, cold butter & sourdough 27
    Anchovies with orange zest 47
    Anchovy & black olive bar pizza 60
    Anchovy dressing 217
    Lamb chops wrapped in paper 151
    Puntarelle with anchovy dressing 115
Antica Formula: Montenegroni 276
Aperol con gin e limone 277
Aperol Sour 277
apples: Apple fritters 245
    Apple tart 234
artichokes: Raw young artichokes with black olives
    & Pecorino 129
Asparagi al vapore e crudi con Pecorino 193
asparagus: Asparagus & saffron risotto 74–5
    Asparagus, raw & cooked, with Pecorino 193
    Egg macaroni with asparagus, peas & courgettes 100
    Fried red mullet & asparagus with parsley, garlic &
        lemon zest 156–7

B

Baccalà alla Livornese 162
basil: *Bucatini* with Pecorino, lemon & basil 84
    Tomato, mozzarella & basil bar pizza 55
    Tuscan basil sauce 213
beans *see* borlotti beans; cannellini beans, *etc*
beef: Beef shin & peppercorn stew 140
    Boiled brisket & tongue with green sauce 173
    Florentine T-bone steak 143
    Ribbons of beef with wilted bitter leaves 161
    Sliced rare beef loin 146
    Tagliatelle with meat sauce 66–7
beef bones: Beef bone broth 202
Biscotti con mandorle, nocciole, zenzero e cioccolato 261
biscuits: Florentines 261
    Moist almond biscuits 241
    Pistachio biscuits 254
Bistecca alla Fiorentina 143
bitter leaves: Bitter leaves with lemon & parsley 123
    Castelfranco & pink bitter leaf salad with aged
        Parmesan 134
    Ribbons of beef with wilted bitter leaves 161

'Black toasts' 28–9
Bollito misto con salsa verde 173
borlotti beans: Pasta, borlotti bean & rosemary soup 71
    Roasted courgettes with borlotti beans & salsa verde 148
bourbon: Boulevardier 278
brandy: Tiramisu 238–9
bread 20, 199
    Anchovies, cold butter & sourdough 27
    Cannellini & oregano crostini 31
    Chicken liver crostini 28–9
    'Not' French onion soup 87
    Rosemary & olive oil bread 229
    Simple bread dough 221
    Tomato & bread soup 80
    Tripe rolls 51
    Tuscan bread 226
    Tuscan bread & tomato salad 112
Broad bean salad with Pecorino 119
Brodo 202
Brodo di pollo 205
Brodo di verdure 208
broths: Beef bone broth 202
    Cannellini bean & cavolo nero broth 76–7
    Prosciutto & mortadella *tortellini* in clear broth 92–3
    see also soups
Brutti ma buoni 237
BRUTTO green salad 120
BRUTTO Negroni 267, 272
BRUTTO Spritz 273
Bucatini con cacio, limone e basilico 84
Bucatini with Pecorino, lemon & basil 84

C

cabbage: Raw white cabbage slaw 182
cake: Sweet grape bread cake 246
Campari: Boulevardier 278
    Milano-Torino 280
Cannellini 185
cannellini beans: Cannellini & oregano crostini 31
    Cannellini bean & cavolo nero broth 76–7
    Polenta with cannellini beans, chard & pancetta 99
    Tuna, white bean & shallot salad 116
    White beans in tomato sauce 186
    White beans with olive oil 185
Cantuccini 254
caperberries: Pork with tuna sauce & caperberries 32–3
capers: *Salsa verde* 210
Castelfranco & pink bitter leaf salad with aged
    Parmesan 134
Castraure, olive nere e Pecorino 129
Cavolo crudo 182
cavolo nero: Cannellini bean & cavolo nero broth 76–7
celery leaves: Cucumber, mint & celery leaves 127

Cenci 242
Cetriolo, menta e foglie di sedano 127
chard: Polenta with cannellini beans, chard & pancetta 99
cheese: Anchovy & black olive bar pizza 60
    Asparagus, raw & cooked, with Pecorino 193
    Broad bean salad with Pecorino 119
    Bucatini with Pecorino, lemon & basil 84
    Castelfranco & pink bitter leaf salad with aged
        Parmesan 134
    Dough ball 'cuddles' with *stracchino* & prosciutto 37
    'Not' French onion soup 87
    Pear with Pecorino & toasted walnuts 48
    Pecorino with melted sugar 265
    Penne with vodka and tomato sauce 79
    Potato, rosemary & Pecorino bar pizza 56
    Raw young artichokes with black olives & Pecorino 129
    Spinach cooked in the oven 189
    Tomato, mozzarella & basil bar pizza 55
    Tuscan basil sauce 213
    see also ricotta
Chianti: Beef shin & peppercorn stew 140
    Rigatoni with wild boar & Chianti 104
chicken: Chicken stock 205
    Chicken with grapes, olives & sage 152
    Fried chicken 155
Chicken liver crostini 28–9
Chickpea soup 103
Chilli & garlic spaghetti 89
chocolate: Florentines 261
    Frozen grapes, grappa and dark chocolate 257
Coccoli 37, 221
cod: Florentine salt cod with tomatoes 162
coffee: Coffee-drenched ice cream with Vecchia
        Romagna 258
    Tiramisu 238–9
Con acciughe e olive nero 60
Con patate, rosmarino e Pecorino 56
Con pomodoro, mozzarella e basilico 55
Condiment di acciughe 217
Condiment di dragoncello 218
Contorni 174–97
cookies: Hazelnut meringue cookies 237
Cotolette di maiale in cartoccio 151
courgette flowers: Deep-fried courgette flowers 40
courgettes: Egg macaroni with asparagus, peas
        & courgettes 100
    Fried squid & courgette 165
    Roasted courgettes with borlotti beans & salsa
        verde 148
    Roman grain salad 130
cream: Spinach cooked in the oven 189
Crespelle 42–3
crostini: Cannellini & oregano crostini 31
    Chicken liver crostini 28–9

Crostini con cannellini e origano 31
Crostini fegatini di pollo o 'crostini neri' 28–9
Cucina povera 109
cucumber: BRUTTO green salad 120
    Cucumber, mint & celery leaves 127

D

Dough ball 'cuddles' with *stracchino* & prosciutto 37
dressings: Anchovy dressing 115, 217
    Tarragon dressing 218
drinks 266–85
    Aperol Sour 277
    Boulevardier 278
    BRUTTO Negroni 272
    BRUTTO Spritz 273
    Godfather Sour 275
    Italian Brandy Flip 284
    Italian Old Fashioned 281
    Lemon & vodka smoothie 253
    Lemon Drop 283
    Limoncello Collins 270
    Milano-Torino 280
    Montenegroni 276
dumplings: Spinach & ricotta dumplings 90–1

E

eggs: Eggs Florentine 106–7
    Hazelnut meringue cookies 237
    Tiramisu 238–9
English muffins: Eggs Florentine 106–7

F

Fagioli all'uccelletto 186
Fagioli verdi 181
Farinata 99
farro: Roman grain salad 130
Fiori di zucchini fritti 40
fish: Florentine salt cod with tomatoes 162
    Fried red mullet & asparagus with parsley, garlic
        & lemon zest 156–7
    Lamb chops wrapped in paper 151
    Pork with tuna sauce & caperberries 32–3
    Tuna, white bean & shallot salad 116
    see also anchovies
Flip con Vecchia Romagna 284
Florentine meatloaf 166–7
Florentine peas with pancetta 178
Florentine ravioli 95
Florentine salt cod with tomatoes 162
Florentine spinach & ricotta pancakes 42–3
Florentine T-bone steak 143

Florentine tomato salad 124
Florentines 261
Focaccia 229
Fragole in salsa di fragole 262
Fritelle di mele 245
Fritte di calamari e zucchini 165
Frittelle di riso 250
fritters: Apple fritters 245
    Rice fritters 250

G

garlic: Chilli & garlic spaghetti 89
    Fried red mullet & asparagus with parsley, garlic
        & lemon zest 156–7
    Small roasted potatoes 197
    Tomato, garlic & oregano bar pizza 59
gin: Aperol Sour 277
    BRUTTO Negroni 272
    Limoncello Collins 270
    Montenegroni 276
ginger: Florentines 261
Gnudi 90–1
Godfather Sour 275
'Granny's handkerchiefs' 42–3
grapes: Chicken with grapes, olives & sage 152
    Frozen grapes, grappa and dark chocolate 257
    Sweet grape bread cake 246
grappa: Frozen grapes, grappa and dark chocolate 257
Green beans with excellent olive oil 181
Green sauce 210
    Boiled brisket & tongue with green sauce 173
Gremolata 156–7

H

hazelnuts: Florentines 261
    Hazelnut meringue cookies 237
herbs: Boiled brisket & tongue with green sauce 173
    Pappardelle with rabbit, lemon & herbs 68–9
    Roasted seasonal vegetables with country herbs 158–9
Hollandaise sauce 106–7

I

ice cream: Coffee-drenched ice cream with Vecchia
    Romagna 258
Impasto per pasta 222
Insalata della casa 120
Insalata di Castelfranco e radicchio rosa con Parmigiano 134
Insalata di farro 130
Insalata di fave con Pecorino 119
Insalata di patate, piselli e cipolline 133
Insalata di pomodoro costoluto 124

Insalata di tonno, cannellini e cipolle 116
Insalate 108–35
Italian Brandy Flip 284
Italian Old Fashioned 281

L

Lamb chops wrapped in paper 151
lampredotto: Tripe rolls 51
Lampredotto panini 51
lemon sorbet: Lemon & vodka smoothie 253
lemons: Aperol Sour 277
    Bitter leaves with lemon & parsley 123
    Bucatini with Pecorino, lemon & basil 84
    Fried chicken 155
    Fried red mullet & asparagus with parsley, garlic
        & lemon zest 156–7
    Godfather Sour 275
    Lemon Drop 283
    Limoncello Collins 270
    Pappardelle with rabbit, lemon & herbs 68–9
    Raw vegetables with new-season olive oil & lemon 34
Lenticche 190
Lentils 190
lettuce: BRUTTO green salad 120
limoncello: Lemon Drop 283
    Limoncello Collins 270
Limoncello con vodka 283

M

macaroni: Egg macaroni with asparagus, peas
    & courgettes 100
Maccheroni all'uovo con verdure stagione 100
Maiale tonnato con bacche di capperi 32–3
Marinara 59
Marsala: Chicken liver crostini 28–9
    Tiramisu 238–9
Martini Rosso: BRUTTO Negroni 272
    Milano-Torino 280
mascarpone: Tiramisu 238–9
meat sauce: Risotto with meat sauce 83
    Tagliatelle with meat sauce 66–7
meatloaf: Florentine meatloaf 166–7
meringues: Hazelnut meringue cookies 237
milk: Rice fritters 250
mint: Cucumber, mint & celery leaves 127
Montenegroni 276
mortadella: Florentine meatloaf 166–7
    Prosciutto & mortadella *tortellini* in clear broth 92–3
mozzarella: Anchovy & black olive bar pizza 60
    Tomato, mozzarella & basil bar pizza 55
mushrooms: fried Tuscan mushrooms 194
mustard: Tarragon dressing 218

N

Negroni con Amaro Montenegro 276
Negroni della casa 272
Negronis: BRUTTO Negroni 267, 272
    Montenegroni 276
Nostrano: BRUTTO Negroni 272
'Not' French onion soup 87

O

Old Fashioned Italian 281
olive oil: Green beans with excellent olive oil 181
    Raw vegetables with new-season olive oil & lemon 34
    Rosemary & olive oil bread 229
olives: Anchovy & black olive bar pizza 60
    Raw young artichokes with black olives & Pecorino 129
onions: 'Not' French onion soup 87
oranges: Almond & blood orange tart 249
    Anchovies with orange zest 47
    Moist almond biscuits 241
oregano: Cannellini & oregano crostini 31
    Tomato, garlic & oregano bar pizza 59
ox tongue: Boiled brisket & tongue with green sauce 173

P

pancakes: Florentine spinach & ricotta pancakes 42–3
pancetta: Florentine peas with pancetta 178
    Pasta, borlotti bean & rosemary soup 71
    Polenta with cannellini beans, chard & pancetta 99
Pane Toscana 226
panko breadcrumbs: Fried breaded veal fillets 170
    Fried Tuscan mushrooms 194
Panzanella 112
Pappa al pomodoro 80
Pappardelle con Coniglio, limone e erbe 68–9
Pappardelle with rabbit, lemon & herbs 68–9
Parmesan: Castelfranco & pink bitter leaf salad with
        aged Parmesan 134
    'Not' French onion soup 87
    Penne with vodka and tomato sauce 79
    Spinach cooked in the oven 189
parsley: Bitter leaves with lemon & parsley 123
    Fried red mullet & asparagus with parsley, garlic
        & lemon zest 156–7
    Salsa verde 210
pasta 199
    Bucatini with Pecorino, lemon & basil 84
    Chilli & garlic spaghetti 89
    Egg macaroni with asparagus, peas & courgettes 100
    Florentine ravioli 95
    Pappardelle with rabbit, lemon & herbs 68–9
    Pasta, borlotti bean & rosemary soup 71
    Penne with vodka and tomato sauce 79

Pork & sage ravioli 96–7
Prosciutto & mortadella tortellini in clear broth 92–3
Rigatoni with wild boar & Chianti 104
Simple pasta dough 222
Tagliatelle with meat sauce 66–7
Pasta alla vodka 79
Pasta di pane 221
Pasta e fagioli 71
pastry 'rags': Sweet pastry 'rags' 242
Patate arrosto 197
Pear with Pecorino & toasted walnuts 48
peas: Egg macaroni with asparagus, peas & courgettes 100
    Florentine peas with pancetta 178
    Potato, pea & spring onion salad 133
    Veal and pea stew 169
Pecorino: Asparagus, raw & cooked, with Pecorino 193
    Broad bean salad with Pecorino 119
    Bucatini with Pecorino, lemon & basil 84
    Pear with Pecorino & toasted walnuts 48
    Pecorino with melted sugar 265
    Potato, rosemary & Pecorino bar pizza 56
    Raw young artichokes with black olives & Pecorino 129
    Tuscan basil sauce 213
Pecorino con zucchero bruciato 265
Penne with vodka and tomato sauce 79
Peposo 140
peppercorns: Beef shin & peppercorn stew 140
Pera con cacio e noci 48
Pesto Toscano 213
pine nuts: Tuscan basil sauce 213
Pinzimonio 34
Piselli alla Fiorentina 178
Pistachio biscuits 254
pizzas: Anchovy & black olive bar pizza 60
    Bar pizzas 52–61, 221
    Dough ball 'cuddles' with stracchino & prosciutto 37
    Potato, rosemary & Pecorino bar pizza 56
    Tomato, garlic & oregano bar pizza 59
    Tomato, mozzarella & basil bar pizza 55
Polenta with cannellini beans, chard & pancetta 99
Pollo con uva, olive e salvia 152
Pollo fritto alla Fiorentina 155
Polpettone alla Fiorentina 166–7
Porcini fritti 194
pork: Pork & sage ravioli 96–7
    Pork with tuna sauce & caperberries 32–3
    Risotto with meat sauce 83
    Tagliatelle with meat sauce 66–7
potatoes: Potato, pea & spring onion salad 133
    Potato, rosemary & Pecorino bar pizza 56
    Small roasted potatoes 197
prosciutto: Dough ball 'cuddles' with stracchino
        & prosciutto 37
    Prosciutto & mortadella tortellini in clear broth 92–3

prosecco: BRUTTO Spritz 273
  Lemon & vodka smoothie 253
puntarelle 109
  Puntarelle with anchovy dressing 115
Puntarelle alla Romana 115

R

rabbit: *Pappardelle* with rabbit, lemon & herbs 68–9
radicchio: Bitter leaves with lemon & parsley 123
  Castelfranco & pink bitter leaf salad with aged
    Parmesan 134
  Ribbons of beef with wilted bitter leaves 161
Radicchio tardivo con prezzemolo e limone 123
raisins: Rice fritters 250
ravioli: Florentine ravioli 95
  Pork & sage ravioli 96–7
Ravioli alla Fiorentina 95
Ravioli di maiale e salvia 96–7
red mullet: Fried red mullet & asparagus with parsley,
  garlic & lemon zest 156–7
red wine: Beef shin & peppercorn stew 140
  Rigatoni with wild boar & Chianti 104
  Sliced rare beef loin 146
Ribollita 76–7
Ricciarelli 241
rice: Asparagus & saffron risotto 74–5
  Rice fritters 250
  Risotto with meat sauce 83
ricotta: Florentine ravioli 95
  Florentine spinach & ricotta pancakes 42–3
  Roman grain salad 130
  Spinach & ricotta dumplings 90–1
Rigatoni con cinghale e Chianti 104
Rigatoni with wild boar & Chianti 104
risotto: Asparagus & saffron risotto 74–5
  Risotto with meat sauce 83
Risotto con asparagi e zafferano 74–5
Risotto con carne 83
romaine lettuce: BRUTTO green salad 120
Roman grain salad 130
Roman style spring vegetables 72
Rosbif 146
rosemary: Pasta, borlotti bean & rosemary soup 71
  Potato, rosemary & Pecorino bar pizza 56
  Rosemary & olive oil bread 229
rum: Rice fritters 250
rye whiskey: Italian Old Fashioned 281

S

saffron: Asparagus & saffron risotto 74–5
sage: Chicken with grapes, olives & sage 152
  Pork & sage ravioli 96–7

salads 108–35
  Bitter leaves with lemon & parsley 123
  Broad bean salad with Pecorino 119
  BRUTTO green salad 120
  Castelfranco & pink bitter leaf salad with aged
    Parmesan 134
  Cucumber, mint & celery leaves 127
  Florentine tomato salad 124
  Potato, pea & spring onion salad 133
  Puntarelle with anchovy dressing 115
  Raw white cabbage slaw 182
  Raw young artichokes with black olives &
    Pecorino 129
  Roman grain salad 130
  Tuna, white bean & shallot salad 116
  Tuscan bread & tomato salad 112
Salsa di pomodoro Toscana 214
Salsa verde 210
  Boiled brisket & tongue with green sauce 173
  Roasted courgettes with borlotti beans & *salsa verde* 148
  Tripe rolls 51
salt cod: Florentine salt cod with tomatoes 162
sauces: Green sauce 210
  Tuscan basil sauce 213
  Tuscan tomato sauce 214
sausages: *Rigatoni* with wild boar & Chianti 104
Savoiardi sponge fingers: Tiramisu 238–9
Schiacciata con l'uva 221, 246
Sciroppo di zucchero 285
Scotch whisky: Godfather Sour 275
Select: BRUTTO Negroni 272
  BRUTTO Spritz 273
Sformato Fiorentina 189
Sgroppino 253
shallots: Tuna, white bean & shallot salad 116
slaw: Raw white cabbage slaw 182
smoothie: Lemon & vodka smoothie 253
soups: Chickpea soup 103
  'Not' French onion soup 87
  Pasta, borlotti bean & rosemary soup 71
  Tomato & bread soup 80
  see also broths
Spaghetti aglio, olio e peperoncino 89
spinach: Eggs Florentine 106–7
  Florentine ravioli 95
  Florentine spinach & ricotta pancakes 42–3
  Spinach & ricotta dumplings 90–1
  Spinach cooked in the oven 189
spring onions: Potato, pea & spring onion salad 133
Spritz della casa 273
squid: Fried squid & courgette 165
stews: Beef shin & peppercorn stew 140
  Roman style spring vegetables 72
  Veal and pea stew 169

stock: Chicken stock 205
  Vegetable stock 208
stracchino: Dough ball 'cuddles' with *stracchino*
  & prosciutto 37
Strawberries in their own sauce 262
Stufato di vitello con piselli 169
sugar: Pecorino with melted sugar 265
  Sugar syrup 285
Sweet grape bread cake 246
Sweet pastry 'rags' 242
sweet vermouth: Boulevardier 278

T

Tagliata di manzo con radicchio 161
Tagliatelle al ragù, tagliatelle with meat sauce 66–7
Tagliatelle with meat sauce 66–7
Tarragon dressing 218
tarts: Almond & blood orange tart 249
  Apple tart 234
Tiramisu 238–9
tomatoes: Anchovy & black olive bar pizza 60
  Beef shin & peppercorn stew 140
  Florentine salt cod with tomatoes 162
  Florentine spinach & ricotta pancakes 42–3
  Florentine tomato salad 124
  Penne with vodka and tomato sauce 79
  Roman grain salad 130
  Tagliatelle with meat sauce 66–7
  Tomato & bread soup 80
  Tomato, garlic & oregano bar pizza 59
  Tomato, mozzarella & basil bar pizza 55
  Tuscan bread & tomato salad 112
  Tuscan tomato sauce 214
  White beans in tomato sauce 186
tongue: Boiled brisket & tongue with green sauce 173
Torta di mandorle arancia rossa 249
Torta di mele 234
tortellini: Prosciutto & mortadella *tortellini* in clear
  broth 92–3
Tortellini in brodo 92–3
Triglia e asparagi fritti con gremolata 156–7
Tripe rolls 51
tuna: Pork with tuna sauce & caperberries 32–3
  Tuna, white bean & shallot salad 116
Tuscan basil sauce 213
Tuscan bread 226
Tuscan bread & tomato salad 112
Tuscan tomato sauce 214

U

Uova alla Fiorentina 106–7
Uva surgelata, grappa e cioccolato fondente 257

U

veal: Florentine meatloaf 166–7
  Fried breaded veal fillets 170
  Risotto with meat sauce 83
  Veal and pea stew 169
Vecchia Romagna: Coffee-drenched ice cream with Vecchia
  Romagna 258
  Italian Brandy Flip 284
vegetables: Raw vegetables with new-season olive oil
  & lemon 34
  Roasted seasonal vegetables with country herbs 158–9
  Roman style spring vegetables 72
  Vegetable stock 208
  see also individual types of vegetable
Verdure di staggione arrosto 158–9
Vignarola 72
Vin Santo: Sweet pastry 'rags' 242
Vitello Milanese 170
vodka: Lemon & vodka smoothie 253
  Lemon Drop 283
  Penne with vodka and tomato sauce 79

W

walnuts: Pear with Pecorino & toasted walnuts 48
  Pistachio biscuits 254
  Tuscan basil sauce 213
whiskey / whisky: Godfather Sour 275
  Italian Old Fashioned 281
wild boar: *Rigatoni* with wild boar & Chianti 104

Z

Zucchini arrostiti con borlotti e salsa verde 148
Zuppa di ceci 103
Zuppa di cipolle 87

ACHNOWLEDGEMENTS

A cookbook is always a collaboration, and I would like to offer my heartfelt thanks to the following people: Brutto Head Chef Oliver Diver. Senior Sous Chef Alan Williams. General Manager Monique Sierra and her amazing team. My meticulous editors Celia Palazzo and Lizzy Gray. My stellar agent Cathryn Summerhayes. Jenny Zarins for her stunning photography, assisted by Kai Gurung. David Tanguy and Al Rodger at Praline for their wonderful design work. Frankie Unsworth and her three assistants, Sarah Vassallo, Georgie Rudd and El Kemp for food styling (and great lunches). Laura Edwards for use of her studio. Annie Lee, Vicky Orchard and Vanessa Bird for their laser-beam editing and proofreading. At Ebury Towers: Lucy Harrison, Catherine Wood, Anjali Nathani, Aslan Byrne, Demeter Scanlon and Claire Scott. Oliver Rampley for inviting me to Florence in 2018 when I first conceived of BRUTTO. Dr Genevieve Verdigel and Emily O'Hare for top tips. All the staff at Palazzo Guadagni. All the monks at San Miniato. And all of Florence's waiters, chefs and bartenders. Couldn't have done it without you.

Bistecca alla
fiorentina

1,15 Kg — £105
950g — £87
800g — £74
650g — £60
500g — £55
— £51
15t

Ebury Press an imprint of Ebury Publishing,
20 Vauxhall Bridge Road, London SW1V 2SA

Ebury Press is part of the Penguin Random House group of companies whose addresses
can be found at global.penguinrandomhouse.com

Penguin
Random House
UK

First published by Ebury Press in 2023

www.penguin.co.uk

A CIP catalogue record for this book is available from the British Library

ISBN 9781529197143

Design: Praline (Al Rodger, David Tanguy)
Photography: Jenny Zarins
Food and Prop styling: Frankie Unsworth
Cover art: Russell Norman (based on an anonymous graffito | found in Venice in 2014)

Colour origination: Altaimage Ltd, London
Printed and bound in China by C&C Offset Printing Co., Ltd

The authorised representative in the EEA is Penguin Random House Ireland,
Morrison Chambers, 32 Nassau Street, Dublin D02 YH68.

Penguin Random House is committed to a sustainable future for our business, our readers
and our planet. This book is made from Forest Stewardship Council® certified paper.

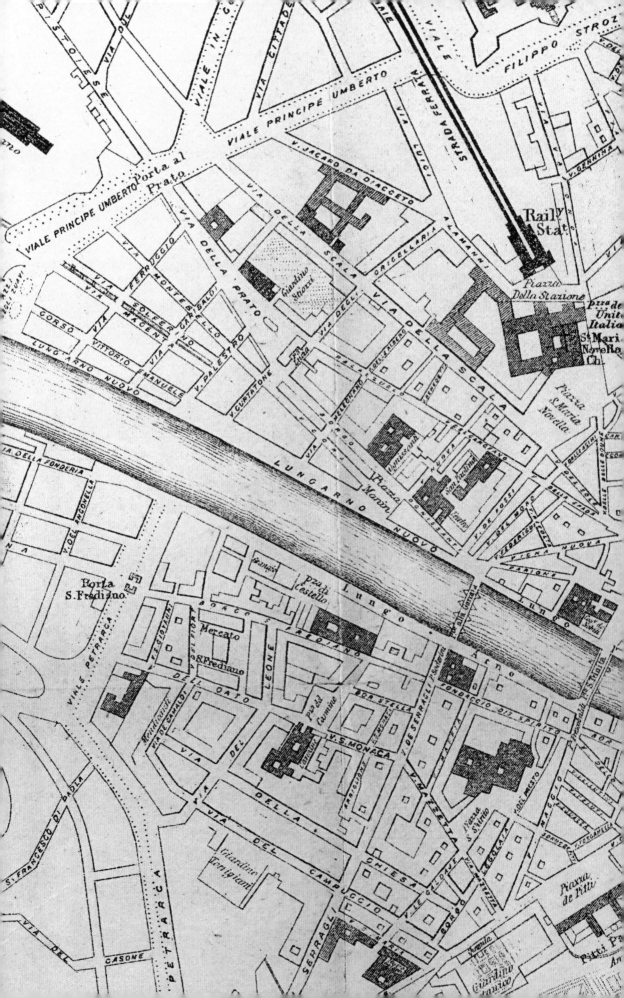